BACK
ON
TOP

BACK
ON
TOP

*A WOMAN'S GUIDE
TO SELF-ESTEEM
AND HAPPINESS*

VICKY BARKER

KOGAN
PAGE

YOURS TO HAVE AND TO HOLD

(BUT NOT TO COPY)

First published in 1996

Kogan Page Limited
120 Pentonville Road
London N1 9JN

British Library Cataloguing in Publication Data
A CIP record for this book is available from the British Library.

ISBN **0 7494 2092 8**

Typeset by *Give-Up Design*
Cartoons by *Lee Kennedy*
Printed in England by *Clays Ltd, St Ives plc*

Contents

Foreword

Have you ever felt 'what's it all about?'

Do you find yourself setting impossible goals and missing them by a mile?

Do you feel it's an uphill struggle and your feet have lost their confident spring?

NO WORRIES!

Vicky Barker has successfully taken the taboo out of self-help books. The journey she has mapped out has courage, wit and humour. Having personally gobbled and digested an enormous amount of self-help books in the last ten years, <u>Back on Top</u> is a must. Start here first, and save yourself - no one else will.

Paula Hamilton, actor and author of <u>Instructions not Included</u>

**Dedicated To Edward
'My Rock'**

Acknowledgements

Much love to Mum whose humour, inspiration and counsel has been unwavering. Thank you for the ten phone calls a day. Promise I won't tell Dad.

Big hugs to my little sister Jenny, whose encouraging words and philosophy, 'Life's too short to stuff a mushroom,' made me keep my thinking in perspective.

Thank you to the gorgeous Jo Newman whose unconditional help on the book was staggering.

Thank you to Stuart Hammersley whose late night design work on the book and calming influence stopped me from completely losing it in the final stages of the book delivery.

Thank you to Gabi Facer for Vision and Friendship.

Thank you to my darling Charlie and Nats who did all the final proof reading and kept me supplied with plates of yummy nosh.

Thank you to Lucy Aumonier, Nathalie Collett, Debbie Lloyd, Michola Neville, Lilias Curtin and Annie Fogarty - The most loyal and amazing friends you could ever wish to have. Sorry the book was a bit like having a baby with you all.

Thank you to all the fantastic people that I have quoted in the book.

Thank you to Lee Kennedy whose humour and amazing creative juices resulted in some absolutely stunning cartoons being produced.

Oh and er. . . thank you to me - after all, I wrote it.

Introduction

In 1992 I was depressed. My career was on hold, my personal relationships were derelict, I was putting on weight - I was desperately out of control. In short my life was taking a nose dive towards the gutter and I felt terrible.

The strange thing was, that this emotional collapse didn't really tally with my childhood which wasn't all that bad. Although I was dogged by bullying at school I had a comfortable middle class upbringing and I consider myself completely normal, in other words, smart, sensitive, I like a good laugh and get floored by the odd million insecurities every now and then. **NORMAL.** So why did I feel so bad about myself? For a while I put it down to one of those mysteries of the mind. I then made up reasons, real and imagined, blaming the circumstances I felt were responsible for my condition: unfulfilled relationships; a disastrous business venture; a lack of money - you name it...anything to excuse what I had become.

One day, motivated by pure desperation, I decided to embark on a course of self-improvement. However, I was soon to find that many of the techniques touted to improve my self-esteem were superficial, quick-fix oriented and had all the explosive impact of a pop gun. Each thing I tried led to failure and each failure led to the next. Instead of feeling happier and stronger, I continued to feel weak and victimised.

Two years of books, seminars and analysis left me convinced that much of the help that is on offer has severe limitations. Whilst every woman wants to know what makes her tick and why - **knowing the 'what' and 'why' doesn't necessarily help if feelings of inadequacy and confusion persist**. Frustrated with a lack of results I decided to conduct my own research in an effort to discover some real and lasting solutions.

I was fascinated by my findings. Along the way I met people who thought they were lucky, who felt good about themselves and yet these same people had been through hell and back several times - physical abuse, sexual abuse and tragedy. True examples of what our character and spirit is capable of. Paradoxically, I found people who 'had everything', a great background, a marvellous education, a loving family - everything that one might assume would provide support. Yet these same people felt like failures and hated themselves with all the passion they could muster.

This insight taught me one thing. The fact that I wasn't enjoying life or didn't like myself wasn't strictly a consequence of my circumstances as I had previously thought, but a 'Confession of my Character'. What is more, many of the methods employed by the 'Quick Fix exponents' fail to account for this, they do not acknowledge that a 'weak character' can significantly impact our levels of self-esteem.

You see, it's not just a dodgy past or the wrong attitude that causes low self-esteem. No way! These things alone do not give a full and accurate picture of our complex situation. The reality is that sadly many of us lack sound guiding principles by which we need to live our lives. This may sound rather twee and old fashioned but believe me, it is **Fundamental Principles** that ensure success. Principles are the basis for self-esteem and it is from them that we find the lasting contentment for our individual life force.

Although today's women share a respect for guiding principles like Courage, Self-Discipline, Responsibility and Activity, few of us display them consistently. We run away from them, for they are ice cold and in this world you must keep your feet warm. We would rather be entertained, understood and indulged; not forced to earn our well-being. Contemplating the moral dimension of our lives is passe for some self-esteem practitioners. It doesn't sell, it doesn't get bums on seats. The self-improvement industry needs to make a profit and it is better to be the 'Quick Fix' evangelist than a rector of the truth. Women of today are busy and they need the answer now!

To clarify the myths and proclaim the truths on self-esteem to women everywhere I set up a self-development company with my partner two years ago. Now I just want to spread information that will help make women powerful and in control of their lives. Nothing I say is new, it's not as if I'm this chick coming down the mountain with tablets of stone, there are no light bulb revelations. My approach is very much 'back to basics' and I make no apologies for the simplicity of my message. All I want to do is to help kick start a new renaissance based on principles, a revival of the 'character ethic' so we can get Back on Top again.

I am not a psychotherapist, psychiatrist, feminist, socialist or any other kind of 'ist.' I am just an average woman on the street who worked out what I believe to be the correct answer to self-esteem and happiness. Of course my style might not be everyone's taste, I am a straight talking kind-a gal. However, I do share a common belief system with you all: I want to be happy; I want to find a sense of fulfilment of myself, by myself; I want to bring up children who love me and I want the respect of my husband.

'Everybody has the right to be happy and everybody has the right to feel good about themselves. To do this you must work on your character and you must build values based on principles'. That's my basic message and I am passionate about getting it to every woman on earth.

Vicky Barker

THE VALLEY OF
CONFUSiON

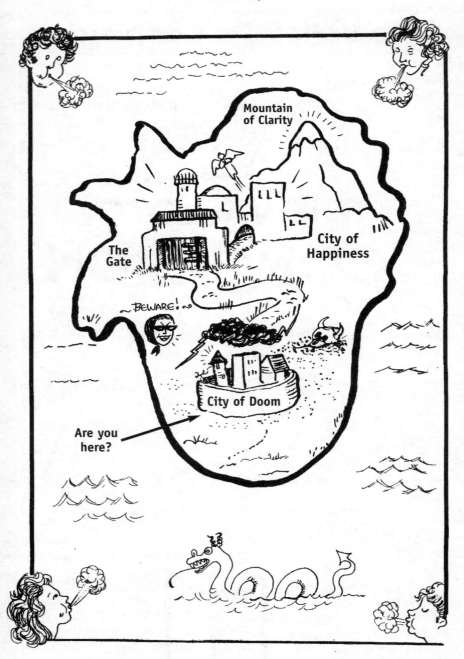

Pilgrim's progress

The Valley Of Confusion

The whole world has gone stark raving mad.

Or is it just me?

At least that's what you'll be duped into thinking if you believe half of the ludicrous labels touted by the so-called 'self-help' industry. We are told by the head honchos of the therapy world that women are no longer dissatisfied with their lives. Oh, no, that's far too simplistic. They are now gloriously **dysfunctional**, and that's official!

Undoubtedly, the trickle-down effect of psychological science, broken marriages, rising suicides, frets about health, worries about dying, general anxiety and depression have made feeling good about oneself the modern woman's Holy Grail.

However, the methods we use nowadays to pursue happiness and self-respect have changed dramatically. Gone are the days when every great society and every responsible civilisation taught individuals to earn their well-being, where principles such as self-discipline, courage, activity, competence and good humour formed the crucible of self-esteem. Modern mental health experts have muddied the waters somewhat since then. We now have to grapple with a burgeoning phenomenon of groovy new identities designed to indulge our weaknesses, riddle us with hypochondria and make us think we're a pork pie short of a picnic.

In our bid to get straightened out the suffering woman can now pay to be diagnosed as either **masochistic, neurotic, narcissistic, hysterical, dysfunctional, dependant, co-dependant and so on.** These labels then hang like baubles on a Christmas tree around our psyches, compounding any feelings of weakness we may have and contributing to our own negativity. A damn good system, if you want to carry on feeling weak, incapable and far too incompetent to overcome your so-called *abnormal* persona. Apart from being completely demeaning, labels like these infer that major brain surgery is your only hope.

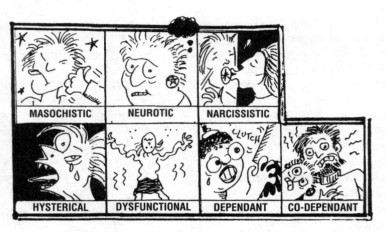

We can now pay to be diagnosed any of the above!

Personally, I have a problem with this. **KNOW WHY?** Because **LABELS CAN DESTROY YOU**. What we call each other ultimately becomes what we think of each other, and it matters.

The reality is that there are big bucks in convincing people that they are dysfunctional. In fact, there is a gigantic industry out there that wants you to be unhappy with the way you look and how you think and we have willingly bought into this. The real tragedy, though, is that although more and more women are looking for ways to feel better about themselves and their lives, much of today's self-help hype is gimmicky and quick-fix.

At the end of the day, the 'pump up' approach has <u>no</u> lasting value, and a few months after lambasting yourself with a splurge of positive thinking, the old feelings of anxiety and unhappiness start to recur.

Why does this happen?

Unfortunately, you can't solve problems on a superficial level, they go too deep for that. Positive thinking and changing patterns of behaviour may well be vital to self-development but they are not necessarily the most important considerations if we want to feel strong, satisfied and happy...consistently.

This is because techniques like the ones above only attack the surface of our dissatisfaction and unhappiness, like papering over the cracks in a wall. By doing this, you leave the deep-rooted problems untouched and the deep internal maxims that affect our perception of life unchanged. You see it's not just our memories or the conscious changes that we make in our lives - a new job, a new town, a divorce - which really shape us, but a long slow mutation of hidden, all-pervasive values; that is, values that are based on solid principles.

Unfortunately one of the essential characteristics of the late twentieth century has been the disappearance of guiding values and principles. As these 'fundamental laws of happy living' have diminished in importance, operating at the periphery of our own awareness, it has become increasingly difficult for an individual to arrive at the threshold of his or her potential.

Look at the logic. If I try to think positively about myself while my character is fundamentally flawed, marked by a lack of purpose, discipline, activity or responsibility, then in the long run how the heck can I ever hope to feel good about myself?

Now for the really confusing part. While the modern day 'ologists and agony aunts crank out 'why-oh-why' theories, it's perhaps germane to note that nowhere in this welter of self-help is it admitted that a girl's **fragile character and lack of principles** could be the reason for her low self-esteem.

Granted, there are no psychiatric categories for laziness, immaturity, cowardice, selfishness and downright stupidity, but even if there were, nobody bothers to consider them any more. This is because in the name of political correctness, in the age of the victim, silly labels and our fixation with the past, nothing is anybody's fault. It's now totally acceptable for people to be weak and unhappy as all our weaknesses can be explained away in a torrent of self-apologetic pyschobabble which rationalises our self-destructive behaviour.

Just stop and think about this for a minute. Can you see what's happening? Our environment is forcing us to live our lives in a way that makes it OK to be weak and a victim. I say it is time to stop perpetuating current conditions that dictate to our lives and find the strength to get back control; the strength to say 'No' when we have to and the strength to say 'Yes' to feeling good about ourselves.

If we continue to make mistakes in our choice of principles and values, we should not expect our emotional mechanism to correct us. If your values are such that you desire things, which in reality lead to your destruction, then you are doomed. Just like a computer you have the power to program your emotional mechanism but you don't have the power to change its nature - so if you input the wrong programme you will not be able to escape from the most destructive desires that you have.

Low self-esteem you see, is not accidental; it is consistent with who we are, our entire character. The principles that subordinate our character without doubt provide our ability, or inability, to deal with life.

What we need, is to start programming ourselves with an internal values' system based on strong principles. It is about getting our confidence, our identity and our security back. And this requires the development of a strong sense of identity, self-discipline, responsibility, courage, humour, friendship, health and so on.

Maureen Lipman:

> I wish I could be full of humour about myself as I am about everyone else. But I'm hard on myself and on my mum and that's probably why I'm in this business. It's a form of therapy. It makes me feel good about myself. It helps me to act out things that frighten me in real life, like low self-esteem or whatever. I did see a psychiatrist for about ten months, which wasn't long enough. It was always the same problem. You tell your psychiatrist how miserable you are and that you can't face getting up in the morning and then go off to star in a sitcom where you have to dress up as a chicken. Now that is madness.

Think of these principles as the foundations of your house. If they are deep rooted and carefully laid then you can build the tallest, largest most roomy house. If they are shallow and laid in haste and without care for the shifting sands of our existence then you will only build the smallest most transparent dwelling that cannot stand the tests of time. If you think you have a weak foundation now - don't worry - you can strengthen everything by re-developing your character based on a principled approach to your future.

THE BIG BOTTOM LINE is that in order to stop the decline we need to stop seeing our lives as a crusade for 'recovery' and we must rid ourselves of the 'victim mentality'. Let us recognise the supreme importance of developing character for creating self-esteem. It is only by doing this that we will achieve the secret to happiness and take back control of our lives. It's what I call the **yes, yes, yes** factor!

You have the right to feel good about yourself and you have the right to be happy. Don't for goodness sake give up that right - you're too valuable for that.

So What's Next?

What we need, then, is not only help with self-esteem but the truth about how we can get it. We want a book that tells us how to put correct principles at the centre of our lives so that we can begin to feel better about ourselves. We want more than labels and quick-fix, we want a book that gives us direction, substance and process.

We also need information about the negative influences which first have to be dealt with before we can develop and strengthen our character!

The City of Doom

The way I have chosen to lay out the rest of the book is to try and make it come alive in your own mind's eye. In **Part 2** I am going to take you to a place called the **City of Doom:** a place where most of us have made ourselves very much at home. A place where low self-esteem and gloom are the norm. A place where there is no vision and people perish. It is here that the negative influences that weaken your character thrive - they are destructive and deadly; they are **'The Character Assassins!'** Their job is to seek out and destroy the traits of your character that support your self-esteem. You will probably know them better by their aliases - **Negative Self- Belief, the Inner Bitch, Foolish Expectations** and **Poisonous Patterns.** All in all a powerful set of dynamos who will obligingly perform a first class hatchet job on any willing woman's brain.

Sophie Grigson
(*Daily Mail* 10 August 1995):

> I'd had a comfortable middle class upbringing and had
> been loved by my parents (cookery writer Jane Grigson
> and critic Geoffrey Grigson). I had also done well academi-
> cally and professionally and couldn't understand why I
> should be feeling so bad. I felt really guilty. For a while I
> managed to find all sorts of reasons: a relationship that
> wasn't working; a bad time at work. Then I realised it was
> the other way around and that the depressions were
> affecting everything else in my life. It was scary as I've
> always been a practical, logical and rational person.

Rather than simply turning us into self-confident hussies, who refuse to be anybody's victim, the Assassins make us feel uneasy about ourselves because they coerce us into thinking in terms of never being 'Enough'. Not good *enough*, accomplished *enough*, successful *enough*, thin *enough*, rich *enough*, or clever *enough*.

In fact, women who live in the City of Doom would rather take their clothes off and swim naked through a lake full of crocodiles than say something positive about themselves. Ask a resident of Doom to list her good points and she struggles and makes her excuses to leave. Ask her to list her bad ones and suddenly, you have a list that makes the Doomsday book look like a dog-eared raffle ticket.

You see, Doom dwellers don't hold themselves in high esteem at all. They inhabit themselves without valuing themselves. This is the greatest obstacle for any woman who wants to progress to a place where happiness exists in quantum amounts.

Until we escape the relentless-ness of the Character Assassins, intense periods of dissatisfaction

Sorry, but you have already fallen at the first hurdle.

and chronic ineptitude in our positive thinking will continue to rule our lives and we will never enjoy the benefits of life to which we are entitled. If you think you can't or don't deserve your dream life, sorry, but you have already fallen at the first hurdle. So start, right now, believing that you do deserve to leave the City of Doom behind you and move to a happier state.

The Gate

In **Part 3,** a natural period of transition occurs, which I have called **the Gate.** Having decided that we would prefer to move to a happier place we start to take active steps to decamp from the City of Doom. This is the first leg of our getaway. In order to get back on top we must move speedily towards the Gate so that we can receive direction and instruction on the way forward into the City of Happiness. It is here that you will find out how to begin the time-honoured task of developing character for self-esteem, success and happiness by unlocking the three Bolts - Self-Awareness, Choice and Reason. This will be your first positive 'breakthrough' as you start to take effective control of that thing between your ears and break with your traditional ways of thinking. Until you take control you will never feel successful or happy, no matter how superficially well your life is going.

The City of Happiness

Once you are safely through the Gate, you enter the **City of Happiness Part 4** and finally you'll be in the position to make the acquaintance of some vaguely familiar friends. These chums are the **Ten Guardian Angels** of our Character. Collectively they represent a series of principles that uplift, fulfil, empower and inspire people. Unlike the Assassins, it's their job to safeguard our happiness and build our self-esteem rather than hack it to bits.

The Angels are not into 'steps' syndromes or programs. They don't advocate miracle cures that promise gain without pain. And they certainly don't hold much truck with the kind of practice that tells you your neurotic existence can be traced back to the day you sat on your pet gerbil when you were six years old. **They don't tell you how to feel differently about yourself. What they do, is advise you how to build a character that allows you to feel good about yourself.**

The only way you can do this is by building a strong and useful internal foundation of principles and principle-directed activity. To this end the Angels give us back-to-basics messages about the key principles that they individually champion. Each one tells you about values' such as Courage, which you need in order to propel yourself forward in your long-term quest for happiness. Discipline: the ability to keep promises and honour commitment. Identity and Purpose: principles that will help you overcome your past by knowing who you are and what you want to accomplish.

And those are just for starters.

By receiving the messages, and internalising their pearls of wisdom, you will discover the factors upon which enduring self-esteem and success are based. This will help you to develop a strong and healthy character which acts as a sort of immune system, repelling any invading 'infections' such as negative self-beliefs, self-doubts and foolish expectations.

So get ready for the secret to longevity of residence in the City of Happiness. And what's more, the Angels can steer you back to the principles of happy living without lapsing into a load of debilitating Californian gobbledegook. Frankly, they're bl**dy marvellous.

The Mountain of Clarity

Finally we will reach the plateau in **Part 5 - the Mountain of Clarity.** From its smooth heights, you will be able to survey all your achievements, and feel justly proud. If we then consistently reinforce these principles as part of our personality and behaviour, through practice and hard work, they become habits. Once new, adaptive behaviour patterns are habitual, they might as well be new character traits. Perhaps they are. You need to maintain on a daily basis all the Angels' benefits so that you remain strong and truly full of high esteem. Anything is possible once you have got this far - your own character is the only limitation to the possibilities.

Helen Keller:

> Character cannot be developed in ease and quiet. Only through experience of trial and suffering can the soul be strengthened, vision cleared, ambition inspired, and success achieved.

The solutions for high self-esteem are not easy, but then nothing of value in life is.

Before you start on the road to happiness you need to realise this golden rule:

There are no 'victims' in character development, only 'students'. A happy and successful life will never be won unless people are willing to fight for it. And that means effort and hard work. Sorry about that.

However the wonderful thing is, that once you start to live your life by principles, in the face of adversity you will still keep on liking yourself and work out a solution without turning your environment into a nuclear wasteland. By getting to know the Guardian Angels of your character well, you will have an invincible army to keep the Assassins at bay - permanently.

TAKE THESE FEW MOMENTS TO REST BEFORE YOUR JOURNEY BEGINS.

Think of yourself as a crusader on a mental pilgrimage - a journey of renaissance - who must fight the good fight to reach your own Holy Grail. Use this book as your sword, your *Excaliber*. It is intended to be an ever-present guide and mentor, to help you understand and forge each stage of the path ahead. All real growth is characterised by a step by step development process. First you need to understand the basic principles that are the Guardian Angels of your character and then you need to apply them. At the same time start to liberate yourself from the Character Assassins and you will become increasingly motivated and directed from within.

I guarantee that, even if you don't already, you will start to feel more optimistic about life. That optimism will be like catching a beguiling glimpse of a beautiful place and knowing, for sure, that not only will you see it in its entirety, but you will have a full, paid-up membership and the right to exist there for the rest of your days. That beautiful place you see is your own new self-confident, happy self.

The road to happiness lies just ahead of you. Put on your mental armour, strap on your sword and leave the safety of your old life behind.

Do you dare to take the first step on your crusade? If so, read on.

Do you dare to take the first step on your crusade?

23

THE CiTY OF
DOOM

part
2

Welcome to the City of Doom

The Assassins

Faith Baldwin:

> Character builds slowly, but can be torn down
> with incredible swiftness.

You've heard me mention the Assassins in **Part 1** and probably wondered what on earth I was going on about. OK. So let me explain. I'm not trying to alarm you, but, as we speak, an incorrigible mob of unruly emotions and feelings are plotting to undermine your confidence and destroy your character. These are the Assassins, it's time to **EXPOSE** them, time to get **TOUGH** and get **GOING!**

Don't think that you can reason with these gremlins - they are nothing better than malignant mind lice. But take a good, long look at them from behind your hands which should be covering your eyes. They have a wicked, shifty glare and like nothing better than to skulk around your head in a sinister, calculating manner. There is a catch however, if you look at these critters for too long, and let them into your heart, they will suck the life right out of you. So you do need to be able to recognise them so that you can fight them, and win.

Character Assassins are the ultimate enemy of your self-esteem and happiness; every time you take notice of these despicable opponents within, you injure yourself. Let me introduce you:

LIMITING
SELF-BELIEF

NEGATIVE
SELF-TALK

FOOLISH
EXPECTATIONS

POISONOUS
PATTERNS
(OF BEHAVIOUR)

The Assassins

Know their names at least as well as your own. They can make you think that the world is a terrible place. The problem is, you probably already feel rather comfortable and familiar in their company. It may well have been a long time since you have known anything different.

This must change!

I call these internal oppressors 'Character Assassins' because their sole strategy is to maliciously attack your character, destroy your self-esteem and slaughter your long-term happiness. All of them have a role to play in well-executed and frequent attacks on your psyche and they help you truncate your vital character base. All it takes is a few seconds and **WALLOP!** In they rush, demolishing all your self-confidence, exploding to smithereens any reasons you ever had for living. Ambushed, I'm afraid.

When we are feeling at the end of our tether with life's little problems, the Assassins simply load their laser guns and zap any rational thoughts, common sense or inner strength you may have floating around. This then allows them to muscle in and take over. You become the host to a whole cauldron of problems, all concocted in your own head. There is no room for any positive, self-esteem building characteristics. And if any of the positive traits do try to raise their heads over the parapets, the Assassins merely aim, fire and shoot them down in flames.

The decline in your character strength is inevitable as they continue to wear you down. Hence the chirpy, galumphing, big-bottomed girl whose life was once a happy-smiley, why-worry beach tragically transforms into the World's Worst Person. Nothing makes an Assassin more gleeful than this dismal mutation.

At Assassin HQ, The City of Doom, the Assassins are sitting around, smoking cheroots whilst planning their next campaign of psychological warfare - it could be you. Let's look at their tactics.

You become host to a whole cauldron of problems,

Their Mission: To immobilise the strength of healthy personality traits, to kill any worthy thoughts you may have about yourself and to take supreme control of your mind.

As dwellers of the underworld, it is wise to point out that the Assassins operate undercover by hiding in the deepest recesses of your mind. Often as not, you are completely unaware that you may have fallen prey to their devious plots and evil ways; unaware that a distortion of reality may have taken place. This is a cold war of the most sinister kind; forget subterfuge, this battle is subconscious.

You may think that you don't stand a chance against such devious foe, but do not fear, I have a plan . . .

Our Mission: Operation Back on Top - to seek out, recognise and zap the Character Assassins where it hurts! It's time they were neutralised, and NOW!

First stage - we must all be thoroughly debriefed in the wiles of each of the Assassins. **Roll the film, Ginger . . .**

Character Assassin 1:
LIMITING SELF-BELIEF

The most natural thing in the world (after eating chocolate) is for your mind to believe in something. Our beliefs control our behaviour, they motivate us and shape what we will and will not do by acting as a perpetual filter through which we interpret the world. When we believe something, **we act as if it were true;** such as there is a God; that the radio works because there are tiny people inside it; or that masturbation affects your eyesight. The power behind anything that you do in life lies in your beliefs. It is <u>they</u> that command you.

Our beliefs can cover a whole range of issues, but none are more poignant than the beliefs that we perceive as facts about ourselves. Some of these beliefs are accurate, such as 'I am a woman' or 'I am tall'. On the other hand, other images whizzing around our brains are hideously disproportionate to reality.

The irrational thoughts that we have about ourselves provide a deadly cache of ammunition that we perpetually bombard ourselves with.

Enter stage left, the first Character Assassin, **LIMITING SELF-BELIEF.** Her job is fire as many negative self-beliefs as she can so that they ricochet around the brain inflicting as much damage as possible.

Visualise it.

The Assassin reaches for her holster, whips out a howitzer and starts to pump you with statements such as 'I am unlovable', 'I am useless', 'I am stupid!', 'I deserve rejection', 'Life is awful', 'Nobody loves me', 'There's something wrong with me', 'I don't fit in', 'I'm not good enough', 'If I love someone I will get hurt', 'I can't trust anyone', 'If people really knew me they wouldn't like me' and 'I'm too fat'.

Blimey, this mental midget sure knows how to start a war!

Once you have welcomed such beliefs over the threshold, they will become permanent residents. All they need is an invitation to enter and in they move. Firmly embedded in their new surroundings, this Assassin is then able to issue unquestioned commands to our brain which are difficult to dispel. The problem is that now you have become certain that these lousy thoughts that you have about yourself are true. Making you feel as hopeless as possible for as long as possible is a favourite blood-sport of Limiting Self-Belief and if left unchallenged, you could soon find yourself her immutable trophy.

WARNING!
You create your reality according to your beliefs. You make your own world. There are no limitations to the self except those which you believe in.

The Origins of Negative Self-Belief

So just where did this deadly Assassin alight from?

Right from day one of our existence, we have been busy learning from others, from magazines and television and from the things that happened to us, whether or not we were acceptable, lovable, worth while, funny, intelligent, talented or capable. Such experiences and subsequent learning provide us with **REFERENCES**, the foundation on which a belief is built. It is these references that help develop our character by having a dramatic affect on moulding not only our beliefs, but our ideas, attitudes, feelings and self-image too. The more references you have, the stronger the foundation and the feeling of certainty that a particular belief is true.

Kiki Dee (*Daily Mail* 30 October 1995):

I had tremendous love and security as a child, which has always given me a strong sense of survival. But at the same time I didn't have a very good self-image and thought that if I could become a pop star, everybody would love me.

Consequently we have references in our psyche that support our self-esteem and ones that help assassinate it! Unfortunately, though, often the limiting beliefs outnumber the positive beliefs as a vast majority of our thoughts are negative, counter-productive and work against us.

So, if we ever get to a point where we aren't exactly over-enamoured with ourselves, then we look to the past for clues to support our Limiting Self-Beliefs. Now you can say, 'SEEEEEE! I WAS RIGHT!', I *am* unattractive, I *am* stupid and I *am* unlovable. Oddly enough, often we would rather be right than be happy.

Let me give you an example. For years I was absolutely convinced that I was pig-ugly (no offence to *Babe* intended). As far as I was concerned, I had plenty of evidence to substantiate this:

References

1 Until my early twenties I had zits so big they had their own central nervous system.

2 My nickname at school was Chunks, and not because of my 'Pebbles' style pineapple hairdo.

3 I was also mercilessly ridiculed for an entire term by a boy I passionately fancied, when a trip to the hairdresser went drastically wrong and I came out looking like a chrysanthemum.

4 And according to every fashion magazine I ever read I was horrendously deformed. The fact I had cellulite meant I would have to walk naked around the bedroom with my bottom to the wall for the rest of my life.

Believe me, I had more references to substantiate my views than a well-stocked local library!

All these experiences enabled me to build a solid belief about myself that I was hopelessly unattractive. This drastically limited my ability to form relationships because I lacked a basic confidence about the way I looked. Of course, not all of my references were accurate, but to fit in with what *I held to be true* I made them so and after a while I no longer questioned them.

Completely oblivious to the trap into which I was falling, I had unwittingly entered the land of the Character Assassins and the City of Doom! By the time the Assassins had finished doing a number on me, I could round up all the self-esteem I had left, place it in the navel of an ant and still have room for a couple of sesame seeds and a peanut.

Thelma Barlow (Mavis from *Coronation Street*, **Daily Mail Weekend 30 January 1996**):

My sister Veda and I were never told to push ourselves forward. My mother's guiding rule was: 'I never praise my children. I always leave that for other people to do'. She thought we would get above ourselves.

Here are just a few typical experiences that can give us a lack of belief in ourselves and lead us to Doom:

- ❤ **Failing at something like an exam, a driving test, a job interview or even a shopping trip (because all the clothes that you tried on were made for Lilliputians).**

- ❤ **Being abused, taken for granted, ignored or rejected especially by those whom we like, love or respect.**

- ❤ **Being left behind on the career ladder while younger and less experienced people overtake you in the fast lane.**

- ❤ **Listening to and believing the media advertisers who prey on all women's insecurities in order to sell more products: You're too overweight, badly dressed, and you don't have nearly enough orgasms!**

- ❤ **Being put down by others or unfairly criticised when you have no possibility of defending yourself (e.g. by your boss at work, or a friend at a party).**

- ❤ **Being made redundant from your job or just getting stuck in a rut.**

- ❤ **The breakdown of a marriage or long-term relationship.**

- ❤ **Making a mistake or doing something that conflicts with your own moral code or values.**

Zoe Ball (*Big Breakfast* Presenter, *You! Magazine* **14 January 1996**):

I wanted to buy a pair of Gucci hipsters and a shirt, but because of my size I thought I couldn't possibly go in there and say 'Do you do size 14?' I always hated going into shops - they can make you feel so worthless.

A word in your ear

Now I'm a little older and wiser I realise the word 'cellulite' is not a term for thighs that look like slabs of Mozzarella, but is in actual fact French for 'a marketing opportunity'.

Napoleon Hill:

There are no limitations in the mind except those that we acknowledge.

Sometimes the references that we have about ourselves can eclipse the truth. At the end of the day, it doesn't matter whether a belief is true or not; it only matters that it makes us feel happy and good about who we are. All of us can find experiences to support our beliefs and be more convinced about them: this is how human beings are able to rationalise. The key question is whether our beliefs are weakening or strengthening our character on a daily basis?

THE BIG BOTTOM LINE

The key is to discover which of your beliefs are assassinating your character and which ones are empowering it. Choose the ones that support you and give you hope and energy. Annihilate the rest.

34

Character Assassin 2:
NEGATIVE SELF-TALK

Sally Kempton:

It's hard to fight an enemy who has outposts in your head.

Many of us have let our self-talk affect our belief in our abilities and what is possible. **NEGATIVE SELF-TALK** is a derivative of limiting self-beliefs and manifests itself in the form of a mysterious and insidious inner voice. Not only do you believe that you are a bad person, you now have lengthy and bitchy conversations with yourself about, well . . . yourself. In short, you have the bitch from hell parked on your shoulder: in her capacity as a Character Assassin, her jaws separate at an angle of 180 degrees while simultaneously pumping out as many disparaging and highly critical remarks about you as possible. A veritable jet-stream of wind!

Times are tough huh, babe? Nobody said it was going to be a bed of roses. You have made your bed, so EAT it! I mean, who do you think you are, MADONNA? What gives you the right to think you should have it any better than the next girl? NO HOPE DOG BREATH! Face facts! Look at your lousy situation! Nobody loves you and it's all your fault!

Jeepers! It's like having a bottle of cyanide wedged sideways in your oesophagus. This Assassin blames you for everything, compares you unfavourably to everybody and sets you up to achieve impossible standards. In her capacity as Chief Bitch, she assumes the self-imposed roles of grand judge and jury and has the uncanny ability to make cameo appearances at critical moments.

35

She also makes up most of the dumb questions you ask yourself and pops them into your mind, rather like dropping a tea bag into a cup. Add a little hot water, finish with a good stir and before you know it, she's got you drinking from the poisoned chalice. **Hurrah!**

She is, of course, telepathic and can read your friends' minds, convincing you that they are bored to the back teeth with you, turned off, disappointed, in fact, generally *disgusted* by you.

T. S. Eliot:

What is this self inside us, this silent observer, severe and speechless critic, who can terrorise us and urge us into futile activity, And in the end judge us still far more severely for error into which her own reproaches drove us?

This 'Little Miss Trouble' is completely *au fait* with all your weak spots and doesn't waste any time reminding you that you always screw up relationships, never finish anything on time and have an ungainly habit of opening your big mouth and planting both feet inside. Believe me, the bitch never shuts up.

Throughout this ongoing dialogue of negative self-talk, the Inner Bitch reinforces your self-directed criticism by showing you greatly edited home-movies of your past mistakes and embarrassments: a sort of 'Jeremy Beadle' selection of nightmare gaffs which obscure any possible vision of yourself as good or worthy. Add to this some special effects to distort your perception of what really happened and pretty soon you have a horror movie on your hands.

So next time you feel a barrage of abuse coming on, grab the venomous vixen by the throat, if you can catch her, and hold her underwater for a few seconds while you turn to your healthy conscience and remind yourself that **you are only limited by your thoughts.**

THE BIG BOTTOM LINE

For most of us, if we spoke to our friends like the way we speak to ourselves, we wouldn't have any friends left. Retaliate against the 'Bitch' and start to appreciate the good things about yourself.

Character Assassin 3:
FOOLISH EXPECTATIONS

Just when you thought it was safe to start living more positively, **WHAM!** you are suddenly lured by false expectations into an emotional booby trap.

In today's world we no longer live in a time where men and male attitudes dominate, dictate, move and shake whilst women just shake and vac. Oh, no! Today's women can pilot planes, perform surgery, run companies and become Prime Ministers.

However, as our needs have moved onto a higher level, our opportunities for self-expression at work and in our emotional lives have created new problems for us.

For a few of us, somewhere out there is the rosy notion that, if I follow the rules or behave in a certain way, I'm entitled to certain prizes: 'I've done what he wants, now I deserve better'; 'I did well at school, I deserve a great job'; 'I did the right things, so I deserve more'. **BIG MISTAKE,** you have just rolled out the welcome mat to the third Character Assassin: **FOOLISH EXPECTATIONS!**

> *To be upset over what you don't have is to waste what you do have*

Kim Wilde (*You Magazine* 6 November 1994):

My depression hit when I was 30, it was triggered off by
the fact that my expectations were not realised. I had
always expected to be married by 30 with two children in a
big house; the fact that I wasn't mattered
more to me than I realised.
My depression hit a low when I was at my most successful
but, at the same time, I was splitting up with my
boyfriend of several years. It manifested itself in weight
gain, I put on a stone and a half, and I drank more than I
was happy with. I also stopped going to the gym and my
self-image plummeted. I was more fragile than I thought; I
felt worthless and ashamed. I had health, a beautiful
house, a family who were backing me and it made things
worse because I know a lot of people would have
died for what I had.
My family and particularly my father, Marty Wilde,
encouraged me to stop drinking and start taking care of
myself. It was difficult but I did manage to kick-start the
next phase of my life. I now have average, uncomplicated
aspirations, such as learning to accept myself, to appreciate my strengths and not destroy myself. I think my crisis
was necessary and probably prepared me for the rest of
my life. It has given me the strength to face anything.

As with Limiting Self-Beliefs, our Expectations tend to shape our external reality. If we expect that people can't be trusted or that the world owes
us a living, then we will find evidence to support these expectations in the
same way that a magician pulls rabbits out of a hat.

A life blighted by Foolish Expectations can also mean that you have to
live up to impossible standards and before you know it, you succumb to the
loony cult called Perfection. The perfectionists are often tempted by crazy
notions like becoming as paranoid as possible about the way they look.
They can do this by buying magazines that tell them that they are no good
in their present state and hang on to every word of some fashion guru who
knows whether their boobies are *de rigueur* or not this season. You can be
sure, they _won't_ have a nice day.

WARNING!

Being perfect all the time is not without its problems. For example, you could be at a party and halfway through the night your boobs might go out of fashion. It happens to me all the time. One minute you're all clamped in, virtually being asphyxiated by a minimal bounce arrangement and by 10pm you're having to strip down and inflate yourself with a Wonderbra. (I'm sorry Mr Fashion Aficionado, but bra-humbug, mate!)

> ## *The greater the emphasis on perfection the further it recedes*

One way or another Foolish Expectations will always end in total frustration or tears because we expected something to be a certain way or to produce certain results and it didn't. Similarly, when you aren't as good or as happy or as successful as you feel you should be, then you feel cheated, let down and start to beat yourself up. On top of this, you start to question your imperfections or limitations and you harangue yourself whenever you fall short of a personal goal. All too soon we get to that stage where nothing seems to work and life becomes nothing more than a graveyard for buried hope.

I'm not saying that your wildest dreams aren't possible, of course they are. But if you don't create an environment in which you can succeed or achieve within your chosen time frame, then how will it feel when you don't meet these expectations?

P D Ouspensky & G I Gurdjieff:

> Begin with the possible; begin with one step. There is always a limit, you cannot do more than you can. If you try to do too much you will do nothing.

If we expect life to be hassle-free, then every time we have a hiccup, it will seem like a disaster: obstructions, tiny tripwires, banana skins and blind alleys are all a part of reality. If you expect challenges in life, then challenges will not cause you frustration. If you expect people to see and do things differently from you, then you will never feel disappointed.

One way to find out what we subconsciously expect to happen is to look at our lives right now, what works and what doesn't. Our problems may reveal unrealistic expectations and our blessings may reveal positive expectations. Once you appreciate the influence of your expectations on your present life then you can take steps to adjust those expectations so that they help you become happy.

At the end of the day, you will save yourself a huge amount of grief if you accept that the planned marriage to Tom Cruise is a bit unrealistic. That doesn't mean to say you have to settle for the blithering, dithering idiot in the oatmeal cardigan either. You don't have to lower your expectations, just *base them on reality*. If you can start to adopt *realistic* expectations about life then you will enhance the probability that your efforts will pay off. It is only positive and realistic expectations that will increase your motivation and persistence in tackling difficult challenges. This is crucial foundation work for character development.

THE BIG BOTTOM LINE

Don't have foolish expectations. Get into the real world. Be rational, you can't enter a marathon if you're not in shape!

Character Assassin 4:
POISONOUS PATTERNS

The final deathblow to be delivered to our character are the lethal consequences delivered by our last Assassin, Poisonous, Sabotaging Patterns of Behaviour. Over time, our beliefs, self-image and expectations compound and we develop certain behaviours. This behaviour can become repetitious and form what is known as a pattern.

Patterns can be very useful. They streamline parts of your life that you don't want to think about. For example, it would be very tedious to have to think about how we perform everyday actions such as cleaning our teeth, breathing or making a cup of tea. Once our brain has learned how to perform these simple tasks successfully, it records a pattern for future use.

None of these actions are done consciously; in fact, patterns of behaviour are not conscious actions at all. Patterns are directed by the subconscious which is responsible for most of the results that we get in life.

There are useful patterns and there are not such useful ones. Unfortunately, some of the less desirable patterns that are allowed to develop can be honed into an art form which drastically lets your character down. Let me explain. You have an 'I am late for everything' pattern: when you arrive, an hour-and-a-half late for dinner, breathless and flustered, your boyfriend knows that he is in for a well-rehearsed excuse of the heavily embroidered, frilly variety: 'Darling, you'll never *believe* what happened: the bus broke down in Oxford Street; so we sat there for *hours* and the driver told us if he could sort the problem he would let us know. Then we had to get off the bus and naturally every cab in London was occupied so I had to walk miles to the tube. Honestly it was a nightmare . . . blah blah blah.' He has just ordered the coffee, so his reception of this likely story is tight-lipped. As you both know, the fact is that you were applying the fake tan five minutes before you should have been walking into the restaurant. Such behaviour, trotted out on a regular basis, puts us somewhere below the dung beetle.

Maybe you have a friend who has drama patterns?

Or maybe you have a friend who is always embroiled in drama patterns. Their life is one big drama. You meet them in the street and make the fatal mistake of asking 'How are you?'. She says, 'Oh crumbs, you'll never guess what . . .', and then proceeds to tell you her problems with all the emotion of a funeral scene from a Greek tragedy. After 20 minutes you've heard enough drama and human interest to keep Coronation Street going for six months!

What about this poisonous pattern of blasting your happiness to smithereens. Let's imagine that you are gripped by a feeling of, Lord help us, happiness. *Now here's the spanner:* you've just remembered that you don't like yourself very much and you begin to feel that all this blatant happiness is highly inappropriate. Your happiness then starts to generate anxiety and a feeling of impending doom, so you create a solution to destroy the happiness you don't deserve. Suddenly you put things off because you are scared, ruin relationships, cry all the time and say things to drive your partner away.

Here are some other common poisonous patterns to watch out for:

- ❤ **Failure**
- ❤ **Accident**
- ❤ **Mess**
- ❤ **Illness**
- ❤ **Financially broke**
- ❤ **Unhappiness**
- ❤ **Food**
- ❤ **Disastrous Relationship**
(why do I always fall for the Bastards?)
- ❤ **'Why does it always happen to me?'**
- ❤ **Sabotaging success.**

Agatha Christie:

Strange things habits.
People themselves never knew they had them.

WARNING!

What you have to remember with patterns is that they can be stronger than reason and often reconcile you to everything but change. As a result, progress and character development has no greater enemy than a negative behavioural pattern.

Once a response becomes an unconscious pattern, you stop learning; in order to change, you have to break the poisonous patterns. Life only changes when we change. There is great skill in deciding which patterns in your life are healthy and which are jeopardising your happiness. This is a question of discerning observation through self-awareness.

THE BIG BOTTOM LINE

By looking back at a repetition of unhappy days, one can see that great monuments have sprung up. However, what you must remember is that poisonous patterns are no more than a fragile noose. . . a noose that can be slipped.

You may well be crying out for some kind of help after witnessing this line-up of reprobates. However, the unconscious chaos precipitated by the Assassins demands to be recognised and experienced before letting itself be converted into new order.

Everything depends upon the psychological place in which we live. If you're living in the City of Doom and you don't like it, you can move any time you like. Break away. Don't tell anyone about it. Others will either smirk condescendingly or mouth sanctimonious babble. Make your escape plans in secret. And damn it, if certain friends desert you, you will find others who have also dared. They will be a hundred times more valuable to you. But before you go rushing headlong towards your new place of paradise, you need to prepare yourself for the move. In doing so you have to pass through a period of transition. It is here that you will receive direction and instruction on how you can get to the City of Happiness. WELCOME, you have just arrived at

'The Gate'.

THE GATE

Welcome to the Gate–
This is the moment when your life must change direction.

The Bolts

Matthew 7:4:

> Strait is the gate, and narrow is the way, which leadeth
> unto life, and few there be that find it.

Life has a bright side and a dark side, for the world of relativity is composed of light and shadows. At the moment, if you are moping around in the doldrums, you are probably standing in darkness and may well want to move into the light. But there is one obstacle preventing you from doing so - it is the Gate. The Gate symbolises a turning point in your life. You stand on the threshold of making a dramatic escape from the shadowy clutches of the City of Doom; through a chink in the Gate you can see the panoramic view of the City of Happiness in the distance with its brightness, open country and happy people. You are so near you can almost taste that happiness, but you still have to pass through this formidable obstacle.

In order to be happy you need to see your situation a whole lot differently and in a totally new way

The Gate has been the stumbling block of many and many more to come. You see, the City of Happiness is not an open door, you can't just waltz in. 'Change' will never be a free lunch, you have to earn it. To do this you need first to understand where you've just come from and then you need to commit yourself to never going back. For this reason the Gate cannot be bypassed; it is a critical juncture which serves not to obstruct you, but to focus you and connect you to the City of Happiness.

In order to get through it, there are three hefty bolts which must be flung back before the Gate will open up to you. It's not just a case of saying 'open sesame' and the Gate magically springs open. No way! That sort of thing only happens in fairy tales!

Pity the poor, burdened-down self-hater who is trying to escape from the City of Doom. Your travels have already been long and hard. But relief is at hand. By unlocking and passing through the Gate you can at last start the process of change. You can stop wasting your life in a permanent state of inertia and turn it into momentum. It is only now that you can begin a journey to the City of Happiness, your ultimate goal.

By the way, it's worth running the gauntlet of a few difficulties to obtain this dream. Don't be fooled, even as you find yourself looking up at the Gate and start to consider which bolt to pull back first, the Assassins will try to persuade you to come back ('You can't do it', 'You'll never be any better than rubbish', 'You haven't got what it takes to be happy'). Or they will try to convince you that they can show you a better way; an easier shortcut. But you must be unrelenting in your crusade. The Assassins will try wherever possible to kill your progress, and when they do, just put your fingers in your ears and push on and forward.

The three iron bolts on the Gate of Change may look a bit intimidating but, like an impatient virgin, they are just waiting to be undone. Each bolt has a name: **Self-Awareness, Choice** and **Reason. These are the agents of change and they are here *now* to help you,** although in the past you might not have appreciated their value too much.

The process of your change begins first with a simple journey of self-discovery. By becoming increasingly aware of how you think and feel, you will find the reasons that are preventing you from having a happy life. Only through **Self-Awareness** can you start to achieve your incredible potential *(Bolt 1).*

Next you have to realise that change is not predestined: you have a **Choice**, to accept or refuse; to stand one side of the Gate or the other *(Bolt 2).* However, because you are only human you will find that all of your choices or decisions will be easier to make if they are motivated by **Reason** *(Bolt 3).*

> ## *It's the most unhappy people that fear change the most*

When you have got to grips with each bolt individually, you are one step closer to opening the Gate. This whole process of taking stock and breaking with traditional ways of thinking enables you to look at your life in a cool, calm and objective way. It gives you control. It gives you a system through which you can begin to change and build your character. The same problems we complained about before, we can now see differently; by releasing The Bolts we have assumed responsibility to resolve them. The invisible forces that surround the Gate of Change know only too well that the difference between accidental transformation and deliberate, systematic transformation is like the difference between lightning and a lamp. Both give illumination, but one is dangerous and unreliable, while the other is relatively safe, directed and readily available.

This is the moment when your life must change its direction. Be afraid of nothing - you have within you all wisdom, all power, all strength and all understanding. **Change is never a loss, it's only a change.**

Bolt Number 1:
Self-Awareness

In order to confront the negative forces that lay siege to your brain and construct a defence strategy against further hostile attacks, first you need to identify what these forces are. The only way we can do this is to scrutinise our Character Assassins by calling for the help of **Self-Awareness.** By finding the reason behind a negative emotion, Self-Awareness can help you take the first step to breaching the wall that keeps you firmly out of the City of Happiness. Of course this raises the spectre that the British most dread: observing and analysing feelings and reviewing the state of your lifestyle and relationships. Still, it's got to be done.

Self-Awareness is simply the ability to stand back and examine the way that we see ourselves. Being able to think about our very thought processes is the reason why we have a fighting chance when it comes to combating our negative emotions. We can all do it. Standing apart like this allows us to monitor our feelings which is crucial to psychological insight and understanding. Need alone is not enough to set us free, we must have a self-knowledge as well. Failing to notice our true feelings leaves us at the mercy of the Character Assassins.

Oprah Winfrey:

> If you are struggling and it doesn't seem to be coming
> together, you can't look outside yourself for why it isn't
> working. You have to stop right where you are and
> look right inside yourself.

A Problem Recognised is a Problem Halfway Solved

You may well find serious self-reflection a bit scary at first because it can be disorientating, confusing and painful. However an inability to look reality in the face, for whatever reason, leads you straight back to the City of Doom. On the other hand the moment you start to become self-aware you stop fighting to stay in the rut and start to get out of it.

John Mayer, a University psychologist in New Hampshire, USA, says that, although there is a logical distinction between being aware of feelings and acting to change them, for all practical purposes the two go hand-in-hand:

> To recognise a foul mood is to want to get out of it.

Mayer also says that he finds people tend to fall into three distinctive categories in how they attend to and deal with emotions.

1 Engulfed

Engulfed people are often swamped by their emotions and are helpless to escape them, as their moods have taken charge. They are not very aware of their feelings and so become lost in them, rather than putting them into perspective. As a result, they do little to escape their bad moods and have no control over their emotional lives.

2 Accepting

Accepting people are normally aware of their feelings, yet tend to accept their moods without trying to change them. There are two variants of the accepting type:

> ❤ **those who are usually in good moods so have little motivation to change; and . . .**

♥ those who, despite their clarity about their moods, are susceptible to bad ones: they accept them complacently, doing nothing to change them despite their distress (a pattern found among depressed people, who become resigned to their despair).

3 Self-aware

Self-aware people are conscious of their moods as they are having them. They have a mature approach to their emotional lives: they are self-assured, know their limits and have a positive outlook on life. When in a bad mood, they don't become obsessed about it and so are able to get out of it sooner. In short, their mindfulness helps them to manage their emotions.

Ulrika Jonsson (The Sunday Times 1994):

My marriage breakdown forced me to confront the past, my relationship with my parents, and ask some very serious questions about myself. I still see a therapist regularly, but I am more able to cope with things and I feel more in control. It's been a mind blowing time, but I'm learning to love my self which I still find difficult.

To create an environment of self-discovery try this:

1 **Stick the kettle on and make some tea (vital in order for a breakthrough).**

2 **Sit in a quiet place and relax fully. Close your eyes.**

3 **Breathe slowly and deeply from the lower diaphragm and go into a totally relaxed state.**

Sit in a quiet place and relax fully.

4 Now imagine coming out of yourself: look at yourself as if you were someone else and observe your thoughts.

5 Think about the mood you are now in. Can you identify it? What are you feeling? How would you describe your present mental state?

6 Observe areas to improve.

7 Smile at the silly things you do, say and think. Laugh at the silly beliefs you have about yourself and your life.

Bhagwan Shree Rajneesh
(*The Tantra Vision* Volume 1):

> Just look next time you are having some trip and riding a problem - just watch. Just stand aside and look at the problem. Is it really there? Or have you created it? Look deeply into it and you will suddenly see it is not increasing it is decreasing; it is becoming smaller and smaller. The more you put your energy into this observation, the smaller it becomes. And a moment comes when suddenly it is not there. . . you will have a good laugh.

Only when you become more conscious of the emotions and impulses behind your actions will you begin to notice recurring patterns in your lifestyle; for example, some of your relationships may be propelled by a fear or anger that you hadn't even recognised before. When you can study yourself in a detached way, uncoloured by your own emotions and feelings, you can start to live life according to realities. Finally you become aware of what you are doing to yourself. The ultimate aim of self-awareness is to be able to stand outside your shell, take an objective peek and say 'Aha! . . . So that's me!'

> *To see your drama clearly is to be liberated from it*

As you go through the awareness process you may well begin to notice that you have a number of counter-productive character traits, such as jealousy or dishonesty, which have been cunningly planted in your psyche by the Assassins. In your heart of hearts, now that you can see them do you think it is healthy to say 'That's me, that's my personality' and then settle for what your traits will allow? Or is it more healthy to try to change these negative thoughts and poisonous patterns of behaviour?

Of course, some character traits will seem easier to change than others. But the thing to remember is that *we can change what seems like the unchangeable*. In fact, often just modifying your behaviour slightly will be sufficient.

An Idea

Keep a journal. Sometimes it's hard to understand your dissatisfaction when it's a formless, unfocused blob. Writing down observations about yourself helps you to pinpoint feelings and identify patterns that need improving. We are talking about your happiness, so make time to do this.

Katherine Mansfield:

> I want, by understanding myself, to understand others. I
> want to be all that I am capable of becoming.

THE BIG BOTTOM LINE

If we allow the Character Assassins to dominate us, they will disrupt our thought processes. So you need to be really sure that what you are thinking is of use and how it is affecting your behaviour. It is the insight that Self-Awareness gives us about Limiting Beliefs, Damning Self-Talk, Foolish Expectations and Poisonous Patterns that will allow us to start taking control of our own lives. That's why it pays to become Self-Aware.

THUD - that's the first bolt thrown back

Bolt Number 2:
Choice

First the bad news. Most people who are besieged with emotional problems think there are few, if any, options. Here's the good news. We have choices - lots of them.

The move into the City of Happiness is a choice, not some predetermined twist of fate. Choice is the second Bolt of Change. Without it, we are compelled into decisions on life rather than deciding of our own free will what to do in a way that is beneficial to our lives.

One of the great revealing facts about becoming self-aware is that often we discover many of us suffer from low self-esteem and unhappiness simply because we don't choose to behave in a way that assumes responsibility for our own lives. In the face of many options, we make bad or stupid decisions. It is in the choices you make that your life is defined.

Consistently making poor decisions reflects a weak character and a lack of sound guiding principles. Without discipline, you'll choose the chocolate cake instead of the muesli bar. Without courage, you'll continue in the abusive relationship. Implied in choice is that the action taken is best, and that all other options are overruled. If we have a strong character then we cannot knowingly choose what is not good for us.

This is why, if you want to build self-esteem and happiness, you must focus on character development because it will equip you with the resources to make the right choices. It will also give you strength to combat the Character Assassins who will have a negative effect on your choices and decisions, or worse still, make you take no decisions at all.

> ## *Destiny is not a matter of chance, it is a matter of choice*

If the Character Assassins dominate then unfortunately, the mere whiff of any kind of choice or decision-making scenario can suddenly unleash a massive avoidance strategy. Decisions about life then become a detachable burden easily shifted onto the shoulders of God, fate, faith, crystal balls, hormones and other influences. Welcome to Easy Street, the main thoroughfare of the City of Doom.

The Truth about Choice

For years, I put my low self-esteem and odd behaviour down to every excuse under the sun. In reality, though, I alone made the choice to feel and behave as I did.

Like it or not, how you feel is not controlled by others or by events. You are not the physical or psychological slave of your parents, husband, kids, boss, the national debt, or anyone else, unless you choose to be. You have complete arbitrary control over what you think, feel and do.

Every day you make conscious decisions. Shall I drink this seventh glass of wine? Shall I take that job? Should I buy that car? Shall I flush my diamond engagement ring down the loo to prove I'm angry with him? Eventually you come to a decision, 'yes' or 'no'. You must then live with the results, happily or unhappily. All the events and circumstances of your life come as a result of the choices and decisions you make.

There is no such thing as luck, chance or coincidence. You always choose. No individual or organisation or Character Assassin 'does it to you' unless you choose to let them. As Eleanor Roosevelt said 'No one can hurt you without your permission.'

If you'd like to know what choices you have made, look at yourself and the life that you have lived. What you see is the result.

In the main, we make three types of choice and these will control how we feel and what we do each day. They are:

1 **Choices that pull you down:** People who follow this pattern tend to complain, blame and get depressed instead of getting on with their lives. Their life is just one big struggle, peppered with negative self-talk and lousy beliefs: in short, women who feel bad about themselves often think losers can't be choosers.

2 **Choices that help you break even:** Most people fit into this category: they make choices but don't really go anywhere; they take the easiest route and their choices need the least thought! Quietly frustrated with life, these individuals avoid making choices that would upset the status quo. In short, they consciously cop out.

3 **Choices that build you up:** These people turn even the smallest of choices into an opportunity. Instead of letting situations get them down, they see difficulties as opportunities to do better things. When one door closes, another one always opens. This is optimism at its most fervent.

Which type are you making?

Blame: The Enemy of Choice

One of the biggest stumbling blocks to exercising choice is blame. Blaming your self-doubt and unhappiness entirely on luck, genes or the stars invariably leads to misery. Whatever your past you can still choose a different future. If you work on your character you will strengthen inside and that's where the pain is. It's worth it.

Eileen Caddy:

> Stop looking for a scapegoat in your life but be willing to face the truth within yourself and right your own wrongs.

If you feel really confused and traumatised by your past, then you should seek professional help. However, many of us are carrying around less serious psychological baggage which we use to avoid a difficult decision. You are not at the mercy of beliefs that developed in childhood unless you believe that you are.

Katharine Hepburn:

We are taught you must blame your father, your mother,
your brothers, the school, the teachers, you blame anyone,
but never blame yourself. It's never your fault. But its
ALWAYS your fault because, if you wanted to
change, you're the one who has got to change.
It's as simple as that, isn't it?

Many women have overcome difficult childhoods to go on to achieve great things. Oprah Winfrey, who now represents for some the pinnacle of wealth, power and success, didn't exactly have an easy start: born illegitimate and abandoned in the Deep South, she grew up on a pig farm and had an underprivileged family life centring around mistrust and incest. Her private conflict over her early promiscuity, miscarriage and battle with dieting has made her *choose* to succeed and her getting to the top is therefore all the more remarkable.

Another of my favourite role models is Evelyn Glennie who turned profoundly deaf at the age of 12 years old. Even in the face of her disability she still went on to become one of the greatest solo percussionists in the world. What most people would consider as an impediment she says is a musical advantage, a gift.

Rather than focus on their disadvantages, these women made a choice to focus on their strengths and abilities. In the process, they developed character traits such as courage, self-discipline, purpose and, in order to succeed, a sound sense of responsibility for their own destiny.

> *You've got to put your
> behind in your past*

You can do it too! You can choose to take control, choose to make the right decisions, even if you know it will cause a little short-term pain. Face facts: the past can't be undone and the future is shaped by our current way of thinking. If there is any value in discussing the past, it is not for its misery but for its lessons and strengths. Learn from it, then move on.

Marie Curie:

I never notice what has been done,
I only see what remains to be done.

Five Simple Steps towards Happiness

Ask yourself . . .

1 Why did i make the choices that i did in the past which have caused me to become the person i am today?

2 Why did i make the decisions that i did in the past to give me the life experiences that i have had in my life to date?

3 What can i do to change? What am i doing that i should stop? What am i not doing that i should start doing? (Focus on character development.)

Then . . .

4 Set a clear solid commitment to make the kind of choices that build you up.

5 Assess your progress by watching the feedback you get from yourself and from others.

Note: Always reward yourself along the way.

WARNING!

Powerful emotions can override your logic!
Remember, when you are making choices about your life, you need to be both:

❤ **reasonable and objective; and**

❤ **in control of your emotions.**

Your ability to choose is your ultimate freedom and must be your greatest power. You have the power to think whatever you choose to allow into your head. So why is it then that we still have difficulty exercising our right to choose a happy life? Many talk like the seas but live their lives like stagnant marshes. There is one thing that commits us to exercising a decision to change, a decision to overcome the Assassins, or do anything in life . . . that is the power of Reason.

THE BIG BOTTOM LINE

You have a choice to like yourself. You have a choice to be happy. Imagine how different your life would be if you had made these choices already.

Congratulations – you're more than half way to opening the Gate. Another bolt has been thrown back

Bolt Number 3:
Reason

It's amazing, isn't it? Here we are, armed to the eyeballs with self-aware-ness, lots of choices and still, when opportunity knocks to make the great decisions, we rarely invite it to stay for dinner. Why is it that, instead of making choices and taking positive action, we flounder like great big lumps of protoplasmic jelly?

You know it makes sense to develop your character because, in doing so, you increase your self-esteem and your happiness. It's logical. But, how many times have you proposed a logical solution to something and at the same time hoped in your heart of hearts that it won't work out? Cute, con-tradictory, and typically demotivating.

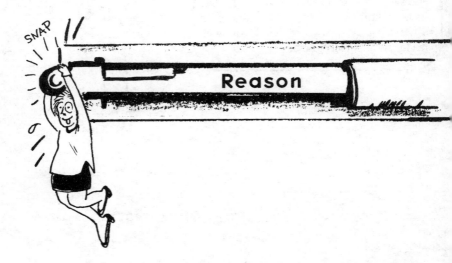

So what makes us so adorably illogical?

Well, often we prefer to be negative about making new decisions as these create change and change causes trauma. New decisions upset the status quo. They leave us vulnerable to failure and rejection.

Remember when the nation was shaken to its roots at suggestions of pound notes being changed to coins and of red telephone boxes being painted yellow! The same fear of new decisions is true of self-improvement: *'You might as well not bother changing your situation, there's nothing out there for you. You'll never succeed and you'll just look stupid!'* harps the Inner Bitch. Much better to make the same bad choices to preserve the *status quo* and just hope that the endurance of misery, with a stiff upper lip, will somehow outwit our inevitable fate.

If you want any form of lasting happiness, best quit this line of thought right now.

The Impulse for New Choices is Reason

No decision or choice is made in life without going through a reasoning process to arrive at what seems like the right answer. Powerful **reasons** are the key to galvanising new choices and new action. Quite simply, **reasons are motivators.** You must give yourself a reason for doing anything in life, from getting out of bed in the morning to doing a degree at college. The only way to stop the lip-chewing, shall-I, shan't-I state of paralysis is to give yourself a powerful reason to change. <u>Otherwise you will hesitate and draw back.</u>

Let me explain how Reason works.

For years, you've wanted to lose weight but just can't get motivated. The nightmares about Rosemary Conley's thighs, calorie counting and colonic irrigation are becoming too much to bear. You are just beginning to resign yourself to a life of lumps and a 'Mothercare' style wardrobe, when the **Reason** for losing weight suddenly walks through the door of your local pub.

He is called Rory, a six-foot three, green-eyed, brown-haired, rugby player. He is absolutely gorgeous and strangely, he thinks you are really cute. **BOING!** The tonnage drops off without any noticeable effort at all. Funny that!

The point is that if you have enough Reason, you can do incredible things.

When it comes to strengthening your character and getting on the road to happiness you have to have powerful Reasons to act in a positive way. It's not a question of capability, it's a question of motivation. It's not whether you *can* do it, but rather whether you *will* do it.

Thomas Mann

Human reason needs only to will more strongly than fate, and she is fate!

Increase the Level of Pain

At the moment, probably the only thing stopping you from passing through the Gate is fear of the unknown. Not knowing what the consequence of your actions will be is more motivating right now than the idea of improved self-esteem and a happy life.

However, if I put a gun to your head and said, in that totally sick way of mine, 'OK, start feeling more confident and happier than you've ever felt before . . . *and do it now'*, then believe me, you would find a way to change your emotional state because my finger, which is poised on the trigger, is a good enough Reason!

The only way you will ever change your current situation is by reaching a level where the pain of having low self-esteem is so intense that you just have no option but to change! The greatest Reason you can create for yourself is the pain that comes from inside, not outside. Knowing that you have failed to be or do what you want in your life is the ultimate pain.

The trick is to link positive and negative emotions to the idea of changing, so that you are driven to making those changes.

You can achieve this by asking:

- ❤ **If I do change, how will that make me feel about myself?**

- ❤ **How much happier will I feel?**

Then link massive pain to not changing, by asking yourself:

- ❤ **What will it cost me if I don't change my life?**

While you are counting the cost, let's just increase the pain a bit more.

Dying to Live

If you died today, would you have done everything possible to have lived a happy and fulfiling life? Suddenly you see the stark reality of what *could* have been but wasn't, simply because you didn't give yourself enough Reasons for being happy.

Joan Baez:

. . . you don't get to choose how you're going to die, or when. You can only decide how you're going to live now.

If you're struggling to answer the question, a sure way to kill the hesitation is to write your own obituary. I know this must sound macabre, but just do this one thing for me: reduce yourself to nothing more than a tombstone, a name and two dates. What would you say about your life now? Get a pen and fill in the space below.

Obituary

In memory of you

Isn't that just the most depressing thing? But often, in the absence of such wake-up calls, many of us never really confront the critical issues of life. Please don't waste your life and let precious days sift through your fingers.

Diana Morton
(the *'Green Goddess'*, on sharing her experiences of cancer with the late Marti Caine, *Hello!* November 1995):

Comparing notes about when our cancer was diagnosed, we found both our reactions were: 'But I've only just begun, I can't have life taken away from me, I've got so much more to do.' Then we sharpened up and focused on what was most important to us.

Unfortunately many people think you have to be diagnosed as terminally ill before you wake up to what you are doing with your life. Don't wait until you are a gnat's breath away from death, get divorced or have some other crisis before you realise that things could have been different. Jump before you are pushed.

It's only when we truly understand that we have a limited time on earth, and that we have no way of knowing when our time is up, that we begin to live each day to the fullest, as if it was the only one we had.

Dusty Springfield
(on hearing she had cancer, *You Magazine*, 28 May 1995):

Strangely enough, it's what I needed. I get stronger with everything that I survive. Suddenly my life is valuable to me and it wasn't before, not in the sense of taking good care of myself, because I don't. But I realised life was precious and I hadn't come through as much as I have not to value it. I have to be taken by the throat and my head banged against the wall to learn what is valuable and what is not. I am valuable, my cat is valuable, my friendships are valuable. The rest is like gravy. If it all goes down the tube, if no one likes the record, I'll wince, I might even shed a tear. And then I'll do whatever it is I'm going to do.

The timing of death, like the ending of a story, gives a changed meaning to what preceded it

Death is a very positive force because it tells you in no uncertain terms that you have limited time. No one gets out of this world alive. But there are some of us who actually believe we will. We act as if we have forever to get things done! 'I've always wanted to write a book . . . I'll do it tomorrow.' I'll give you a tip: *you might not.*

Helen Storey, the award-winning fashion designer, has faced some intense battles in recent years. In 1993 her husband was diagnosed as having cancer and in 1995 her business had been put into administrative receivership. In a newspaper article, she talked about her reaction to her personal and professional crisis (*Daily Mail* 22nd June, 1995):

People say I've got stronger than I was before, but I don't recognise it as a strength, I see it as bloody-mindedness. The energy I've gained from nearly having my life blown to bits means I want to do good not only for myself but for other people who go through the same things as me, professionally as well as personally. I can't stand waste now, whether that's waste of talent in myself or other people.

Live as you would have wished to have lived if you found out you were dying tomorrow. Get passionate about the important things, don't waste time worrying about the ephemeral.

It's not enough just to ask yourself what you want to be. Ask yourself *why* you want to be it. Without a 'why' you have no guide, no reason to go for these things. It is only the 'why' that will command you to go on and fulfil your dreams.

Confine yourself to the present - do it now!

The past is **dead**. The future is **imaginary**. Happiness can only be found in the **now.** Your life is not a dress rehearsal, don't let death stare you in the face before you realise this. The future doesn't exist, it's just a figment of our imagination. It's the potential of the present that counts. So, don't postpone your better future, do it all now. You've got to have lots of strong reasons why the change should take place immediately, not some day in the future.

**If you don't make the change now, then you
don't have enough Reasons.**

Life is not a dress rehearsal

if i Had My Life Over

I'd like to make more mistakes next time.

I'd relax, I'd limber up.

I would be sillier than I have been on this trip.

I would take fewer things seriously.

I would take more chances.

I would climb more mountains and swim more rivers.

I would eat more ice cream and less beans.

I would perhaps have more actual troubles, but I would have fewer imaginary ones.

You see I'm one of those people who live sensibly and sanely hour after hour day after day.

Oh, I've had my moments, and if I had to do it again, I'd have more of them. In fact, I'd try to have nothing else. Just moments one after the other instead of living so many years ahead of each day.

I've been one of those persons who never goes anywhere without a thermometer, a hot water bottle, a raincoat, and a parachute.

If I had to do it again, I would travel lighter than I have.

If I had to live my life over, I would start barefoot earlier in the spring and stay that way till fall.

I would go to more dances.

I would ride more merry go rounds.

I would pick more daisies.

Nadine Stair (aged 85)

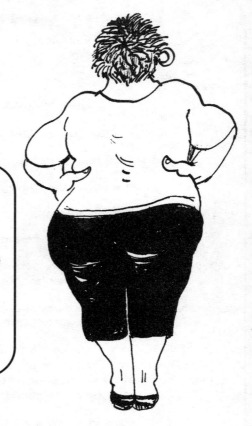

THE BIG BOTTOM LINE

Carpe diem, seize the day, and find a reason to change now!

Life is Just Sudden Death Overtime, and the clock is running.
No Fear **T-shirt caption**

The three Bolts which open the door to change have now been released and thrown back. You touch the Gate lightly and marvel at how easily it responds to your hands. Your first few momentous steps through the Gate should be moments to savour. You have gained mastery over three very important tools which will begin to construct the backbone of the new you.

Choice, Reason and Self-Awareness are now at your command.

You are finally ready to enter the City of Happiness...

THE CiTY OF
HAPPiNESS

part 4

With a resounding thud, the Gate has closed behind you

The Angels

With a resounding thud, the Gate has closed behind you. Take a deep breath and feel very proud. You've finally made it through the Gate but you're feeling all alone and more than a little bit scared. Perhaps you thought you would feel more confident, more in control already. But you have to realise that you have never been this far into your psyche before and it's a landscape you don't recognise. How could you? The Assassins have never let you get this far before.

There are few landmarks to feel familiar with, no Self-Doubt ledges to leave your excuses on, no Negative Self-Images to mirror your worries, no Poisonous Pattern beanbags to flop onto. Now the Gate has slammed shut, you may feel even less confident than in the City of Doom. Where is the light to help you find your way? Where are the familiar faces of the Assassins? Realise straight away that although this is certainly not quick-fix city, it is the beginning of the road to long-term happiness.

You may think that getting through the Gate was the most difficult decision that you had to make. You were right. At this stage, you are tottering on a precipice, but fear not! You are not alone, for waiting in the wings (excuse the pun) is your own personal host of Guardian Angels.

At this stage, you are tottering on a precipice, but fear not!

These excellent cohorts are a group of solid principles who are just waiting to spring into action and fight valiantly against the evil Character Assassins. Individually strong, *en masse* they are invincible. Frankly, those dastardly Assassins don't stand a chance against your own in-built Character Army. The Angels will give you strength through the transition from shaky changeling, 'I am no longer at the beck and call of my own Character Assassins', to strong and feisty Confidence Queen, 'I am responsible for my own life and I am the only one that can change it.'

There are ten of these gems at your disposal, let me introduce you to them:

These Angels come knocking on the doors of our hearts and minds trying to deliver a vocal message to us via our healthy conscience. They couldn't have opened the Gate for you, but thankfully you listened through the cordon for those Angels, then threw open the three Bolts and opened up that Gate. What does the Angel do then?

An Angel never says 'Hello'. You reach out and take the message, and the Angel gives you your instructions, encouraging you to move forward: 'Get up and sock it to em' Babes!' Then the Angel flies away. From now on it is your responsibility to take action.

The Angels work best as a team. As one Angel gives you information and guidance on how to develop a 'happiness trait' it reinforces the development of other traits. You have the power to summon this Army of Angels. They are inside. Your side. With their help you can make more informed choices which will enable you to get Back on Top. Don't worry if these principles of happiness have been dormant up until now because of all the negative dialogue you have been pumping yourself with. It simply means that when you finally wake them up you will be more refreshed.

You have already made the most important choice of your life to date, to traverse the portico of the Gate and begin the road to true self-worth. Let's now listen to the messages of the Angels in more detail, you need to get to know them better than you got to know the Assassins. How else will you feel truly equipped to grind the Assassins into the dust once and for all?

Guardian Angel 1:
RESPONSIBILITY

Family, friends, teachers, self-help books and the Samaritans can only give you so much advice. They can put you onto what they think is the right path, but the final forming of your character lies in your own hands. 'That's just the way I am' is not an excuse for pathetic behaviour. Nor is it correct, because we are never just what we are. As Aristotle was among the first to insist, *'We become what we are as persons by the decisions that we make ourselves'.*

Let's dissect your first Guardian Angel, **RESPONSIBILITY** - 'response-ability' - the ability to choose your response. Happy and successful women recognise that responsibility is something to be proud of rather than something to avoid. In her capacity as a ministering spirit, Responsibility allows you to assume full control of your own emotions, decisions and actions, rather than allowing external forces or Assassins to manipulate you.

With Responsibility on your side you take control and stop waiting for others to fulfil your dreams. If there is a problem, Responsibility makes you ask, 'What can I do about it?'; 'What avenues of action are open to me?' And if something goes wrong, you stop yourself from indulging in orgies of blaming. In short, you take responsibility for your own existence.

Anita Baker:

> I say if it's going to be done, let's do it. Let's not put it in the hands of fate. Let's not put it in the hands of someone who doesn't know me. I know me best. Then take a breath and go ahead.

How the Assassins Kill Responsibility

If you don't take responsibility for yourself, then you are easy prey for the Assassins. Once they get their grubby little hands all over that expansive mind of yours, they can twist your thoughts so that the idea of having no responsibility at all seems like a great strategy. Making excuses becomes a way of life and of course, nothing is ever your fault. And you end up making the fatal mistake of confusing bad luck with destiny.

As the woman who avoids responsibility surrenders to the unfolding dramas in her life, her archetypal response is 'Oh, maybe it's just meant to be'. She, of course, is addicted to astrology and would be mortified if she ever discovered that her fate was not, in fact, controlled by pivotal positions of the planets after all, but nothing more astral than herself. She loves being able to justify her miserable existence, refuting the fact that she could ever be responsible for her own unhappiness. She is an expert in finding scapegoats to legitimise her sorry state. **Blame - justify - blame - justify.** She finds this a breakthrough formula for passive living.

> *The people who get on in this world are the people who get up and look for the circumstances they want, and, if they can't find them, they make them.*

The breakthrough, of course, quickly reverts to a breakdown, as she completely loses control of her life. What everyone has omitted to tell her (of course it's not her fault she didn't know) is that *self-esteem and happiness are an inside job*. And that she alone is responsible for these things. Nevertheless responsibility seems a bit too much effort for her liking, no hooks to hang the well-seasoned excuses on, and so on.

Taking responsibility would mean that she would have to give up feeling sorry for herself; to stop blaming her parents for everything. She would probably have to start exercising, stop wallowing in self-pity and get off her arse and do something. But the worst thing would be to forfeit the sympathy of others and let people know she was happy . . . This would never do. The Assassins wouldn't stand for it.

When you have the Angel of Responsibility on your side, like a true friend she gives it to you straight. She makes you understand that the reality of our existence is that we are on our own.

'The buck stops right here'

"This whole life thing is a one-woman tango, sister."

75

The truth is that other people are too busy trying to work out their own lives to be really bothered with your unhappiness. Harsh but true.

Girls who don't take responsibility are always looking for sympathy; instead they get pity. If they took responsibility that pity would turn into respect.

In order to get on and take responsibility, you've got to stop seeing yourself as the victim of the universe. Responsibility is simply the basis of our individual determination to accept life and fulfil ourselves within it. You've got to be able to say to yourself 'the buck stops right here' and 'I'm not content to live like this any more'. If you can do this, your self-esteem will improve automatically because you'll feel strong and responsible rather than powerless and victimised.

Being Overly Responsible

The woman that is too responsible always puts others' needs before her own. She is a sort of St Joan of the Fitted Units and is always ready to throw out a sympathetic apron string to anybody who bears that needy look.

Always ready to throw out a sympathetic apron string.

Alice Walker:

> Not everyone's life is
> what they make it.
> Some people's life is what
> other people make it.

She happily gives up her life for her husband, kids, family, friends and boss because, as the Assassins constantly remind her, to be unselfish and of service is what nice people do, isn't it? She forgoes her life's ambition of digging up fossils in China in favour of digging other people out of their holes instead.

It's wise to remember that over-responsibility in one person always leads to under-responsibility in the other person. Never do something for someone else that they are capable of doing themselves. You are not in charge of their feelings, problems, needs, tasks, meals, clothing, homework, hangovers, hang-ups, important decisions and illnesses.

So what happens when you become too responsible?

The short answer is, you get ill. When you repress your emotions, usually so that you can deal with everyone else's, your body keeps score. Women who are too responsible have very dangerous rules that start with the prefix have to . . . should do . . . need to . . . or supposed to . . . In the end you spend most of your days doing what you don't want to do in order to keep everyone else happy, holding yourself responsible for matters beyond your control. This is a high risk strategy, **Olivia Newton-John** explains why:

I was told about breast cancer on the same day as my father's death. I had a squeaky clean and healthy life; no booze, no cigarettes, I was a veggie for years and I exercised everyday. But I had been under a lot of stress trying to take care of everybody. If ever I was troubled I would suppress my emotions and push my 'upset feelings' down.
I wouldn't let people know if I was angry because I had this good girl nice girl image and wasn't supposed to get angry.
It's unhealthy to push it down.
I went to a therapist the day after I was diagnosed with cancer and the first thing she said to me was 'you haven't been taking care of yourself, it sounds like you have been breast-feeding everybody. You want to let them go, you've got to wean people off you.'
It was a revelation for me, the message was take care of myself first before putting everybody else before me. It's a bad thing we are taught in society, especially with women, that taking care of yourself is a selfish thing.

Giving your life to others is effectively allowing them to control your life. It's a bit like giving a chimpanzee a Ming vase to play with. This eventually translates into anger and bitterness because you never get the chance to live out who you really want to be. The reality of this waste really hits home when, for example, you have spent years identifying with the role of being a mother and your child finally flys the nest. Or when a marriage ends in divorce. Or your partner dies. Or you lose a job that you have given your life to. Now that these people are no longer dependent on you, **WHO ARE YOU?**

Robin Norwood:

We achieve a sense of self from what we do for ourselves and how we develop our capacities. If all your efforts have gone into developing others you are bound to feel empty.

TAKE YOUR TURN NOW!

To 'take your turn' you need summon up the Angel and assume responsibility for your own world by thinking in terms of specific action.

What action can I take:

- ❤ **that will bring me closer to my goal?**

- ❤ **to become a better lover?**

- ❤ **so I stop feeling so guilty all of the time?**

- ❤ **to become happy?**

- ❤ **to advance my career? to raise my income?**

- ❤ **to preserve my identity?**

Action springs not from thought, but a readiness for responsibility

Work on yourself and think how more valuable you'd become; think what that would do for family and friendships as well as yourself. Self-sacrifice creates low self-worth, while self-development creates self-esteem.

Bhagwan Shree Rajneesh:

> If you depend on someone for your happiness you are
> becoming a slave, you are becoming dependent, you are
> creating a bondage and you depend on so many people;
> they all become subtle masters, they all exploit
> you in return.

If it's to be, it's up to me

If you take complete responsibility for your
life, you'll have control. I suspect, if anything,
most of us oscillate between being under-
responsible and over-responsible. If you
become too responsible in one area of your
life you tend to go to the other extreme
both as a way of dealing with the pressure
of responsibility and as a way of trying to
redress the balance.

Well-balanced self-responsibility is a
powerful experience that brings your life
back into the palm of your hands. Look at
your life and assess your levels of responsibility in different areas. You could be very
responsible at work and very irresponsible at
home. You could be very responsible about money
and totally irresponsible with your health. You may be
very active in making sure everyone else is happy and at
the same time completely disregard your own emotions.

Your life back into the palm of your hands.

Invariably you will have to make new decisions in life that you won't like,
and others won't like, but you have to make them and then suffer the consequences. It's what 'being a grown-up' is all about.

THE BIG BOTTOM LINE

Your most radical transformation will occur when
you realise that no one is coming to the rescue
and while you're at it, ditch the halo, girls, it's
only another bloody thing to keep clean.

Guardian Angel 2:
COURAGE

It was sunny, but she thought it was dark. The air was chilly, but she did not feel the cold. The guns were still pounding, but to Major Rhonda Cornum, the desert seemed eerily quiet. She had been badly injured but nothing hurt: for a fleeting moment, she even thought she might be dead. Then she looked up, saw five Iraqi soldiers standing over her, holding guns, and came back to life enough to realise that she had been captured by the enemy.

With both arms badly broken, a smashed knee, a crushed hand, a bullet wound to the shoulder and a number of gashes all over her body, Rhonda was taken into captivity, sexually assaulted and held for eight days as a prisoner of war.

In one of the least-known episodes of the Gulf War, American Army doctor **Rhonda Cornum,** a 36-year-old wife and mother of a 14-year-old girl says this of her ordeal:

> I was so fortunate not to be dead: anything that was going to happen was better than that. There was no time for fear. Fear is something that happens when you just sit around and stew.
> **Daily Telegraph, 16 January 1996**

Fear is something that happens when you just sit around and stew.

The priceless Angel of Courage was Major Rhonda Cornum's salvation. This account of her harrowing experiences and subsequent bravery is inspirational in the extreme. I started this chapter with her story, not to be sensationalist but because she makes one heck of a valid point about life: fear happens when you have the time to think about the consequences of your actions. You need the Angel of Courage to overcome it. Courage is the ability to overcome fear and move into action. It's a Principle we must develop and is the foundation upon which all other guiding principles rest.

We Need Courage to Act

Most of us start life with an abundance of courage. As children, we're fearless and we enjoy taking risks. However, we are continually discouraged from doing so, as our parents attempt to protect us from the outside world. But it's hard to develop courage in a society where our whole way of life is dedicated to the removal of risk. Our preoccupation with being 'safe and secure rather than sorry' borders on the obsessive. From cradle to grave we are supported, insulated and isolated from all the risks in life. And if we fall? Then everyone, from governments to therapists, are on stand-by, ready with the social aspirins and Band-Aids.

As children, we're fearless

The world is a scary place but, by cocooning ourselves from the harsh and unpredictable realities of life, we are actually desensitising ourselves from the need for human experience. Far too many of us are spending night after night cooking our brains in front of the TV, handing our right to excitement over to the celluloid soap opera stars. Not very nourishing for the mind, but an excellent source of bubblegum for the eyes.

> *We cannot discover new oceans*
> *unless we have the courage to lose*
> *sight of the shore*

Fear and Self-Loathing

Speaking personally, my hyperbolic propensity to fret about life established me as the first woman in the world to have clenched hair. OK, so I exaggerate a little. However one fact is that, as a professional worrier, I am far from unique, nearly all of us stew over a wide variety of fears; these include money worries, criticism, ill health, lost love, old age, death, rejection, loss of identity, stressful change and the economy. These fears are nearly always totally irrational. So why do we worry? Well, in virtually all cases, our fears are acting as a defence against free-floating anxieties about ourselves.

Self-doubt and a lack of trust are completely normal emotions, no matter how irrational they are. The tough bit is learning to face them. But you have to do it in order to have courage.

But what is F E A R ?

F **alse**

E **vidence**

A **ppearing**

R **eal**

> ## Fear is nothing more than a state of mind

What you think affects your whole being. The mind can be a great source of terror or of great power and inspiration. Examine your thoughts and ask yourself if there is any basis in reality for this thought process. Don't let your mind terrorise you. Catch the Assassins in action and refuse to listen to them.

The more insecure or self-doubting we are, the more likely we are to turn any victory into defeat so that we reinforce our own feelings of incompetence, inadequacy and unworthiness.

So if you really want to get rid of the fear of doing something, it's simple; go out and . . .

Just Do It!

. . . and panic later. The only way to overcome fear, as any courageous Angel will tell you, is to experience it and work through it. Often, fear of particular situations will evaporate when confronted. Let me illustrate from personal experience.

My big anxiety in life was a crippling fear of public speaking. One night I was out with a girl friend and after a few drinks (need I say more) she got me to agree to do a little talk to her company on 'success' techniques. 'No problem!' I slurred, with all the confidence of somebody who had just downed four glasses of Chardonnay. The next morning she phoned me to remind me of my commitment. 'Of course I remember', I said, trying not to let the blind terror in my voice show through. I was now committed to a confrontation with my worst nightmare and there was no backing out.

The entire week preceding the 'talk', the Assassins did their utmost to try to get me to cancel, by tormenting me with continuous what if's: what if I go into an uncontrollable, hysterical fit followed by an epileptic seizure?

What if I have a clump of spinach wedged between my teeth? What if my dress falls off?

The fateful day came soon enough. When I finally got up to speak, you could stir my knees with a spoon, my heart felt that it was going to burst through my jacket while the Inner Bitch carped helpfully, 'You're doomed'. I froze solid. Then I gave myself a stern talking to and posed a question, the answer to which was the catalyst that unlocked my courage. The question was:

'What will i feel like after i've done this?'

How will I look like after I've successfully completed the seminar? I then conjured up an image of me: ecstatically happy, proud and brimming over with self-respect. Yes! If I could only get through the next hour, I knew that the courage to conquer my worst fear would set me free to do anything I wanted.

The inner Bitch carped helpfully, 'You're doomed'.

With this in mind, I felt an enormous surge of fear but . . . I did it anyway. Result? One massive step of the courageous kind.

After all the palaver, I was fine. I am thrilled that I did it. And now, quite frankly, I'm insufferable.

Go On, Risk It! What Have You Got to Lose?

The best antidote to fear is to be as daring as possible and this means taking a few risks. To do anything in life is risky. To fall in love can be a massive risk. But risk must be taken because the greatest hazard of life is to risk nothing. The person who risks nothing does nothing, has nothing, is nothing.

If we sacrifice courage for a secure and settled life, where nothing can happen to us, then we deny life itself. You must have the courage to do things, regardless of the consequences. Brave actions inspire bravery.

Women Who Risked it and Won

❤ **Elle Macpherson,** on facing the critics for her debut in *Sirens*:

'It could have been a total disaster. It was a gamble, but you don't get anything in life if you don't change.'

❤ **Waris Dirie,** the newest edition to the supermodel clan, walked barefoot through the desert:

'I can't say how long I travelled, but I was determined to escape the life of servitude my mother and her mother had endured.'

❤ **Elizabeth Hurley:**

'The more I do, the more I'm prepared to take risks and not play safe, to go all out to do something that makes me shudder just at the thought of it.'

❤ **Meg Ryan:** Risk meant acting the legendary orgasm scene in *When Harry Met Sally*:

'After you do a scene like that it seems very risky and you think, "Oh my God, what did I just do?"'

Pushing through fear is less frightening than living with the underlying fear that comes from a feeling of helplessness and boredom, produced by the absence of risk. All you have to do so as to diminish your fears is develop more trust in your ability to handle whatever comes your way. You want to achieve a level where you can say: whatever happens to me, given any situation, I can handle it!

i can handle it!

Amelia Earhart:

> Please know that I am aware of the
> hazards. I want to do it because I want to do it. Women
> must try to do things as men have tried. When they fail,
> their failure must be but a challenge to others.

WARNING !

A courageous person is one who overcomes fear and takes calculated risks in order to move forward, not to be confused with one who is stupid enough to have no fear at all. Courage is not the absence of fear, it is the control of fear.

. . . And Keep Doing It

When you finally push through the fear which is preventing you from being happy, it's not enough to confront it once. You have to keep doing it. You have to keep facing fears, taking stands and acting bravely, even when you don't really feel brave. Courage is like a muscle which is only strengthened with use. Only when you act with courage does that courage develop into an integral part of you.

Use Your Disasters to Learn Courage

Never let a thumping good disaster go to waste. You may not have looked at life like this before, but believe me, disaster, mistakes, failure and major trauma are the coolest bunch of teachers in town. Without them, you learn absolutely nothing about the value of life, how to make better choices or how to become a stronger, more courageous person.

Olivia Newton-John
(Talking on Australia Channel 9 network, September 1994):

The night after I was told I had cancer, I woke up at about
two o'clock in the morning, and went downstairs, I had
never felt so frightened. It was the fear of not knowing
what's going to happen. At that point I still didn't know
exactly what they were going to do. I felt real terror for a
little while. I had to make a decision then. I had to decide:
'Do I go along with this or do I really fight it?'
Your mind is a very strong, very powerful thing.
You can make things real in your own mind.
It sounds ironic to say that breast cancer is probably the
best thing that happened to me, but I really think it was.
It made me grow up a lot, it made me work out my priori-
ties and it made me let go of a lot of fears and a lot of
things that I didn't need to be doing and that
I felt I had to be doing.

A bad experience is not what happens to you; it's what you do with it.
You can wallow in defeat or turn the experience into a resounding victory.
If you want to succeed in staying in the City of Happiness be prepared to
keep facing failure or disasters courageously. This is the only way you
learn; every time you learn you create a chance to succeed. See everything
as a learning experience. Not only does this make you feel better because
you don't see yourself as a failure; you also learn never to be afraid of failure or disasters.

THE BIG BOTTOM LINE

Be bold and courageous. When you look
back on life, you will regret the things
that you didn't do more than the things
that you did. But you don't need to wait
until a crisis arises. Start now.

Guardian Angel 3:
HEALTH

John Locke:

A sound mind in sound body is a short but full description of a happy state in this world.

Healthiness equals happiness. You need the energy and vitality provided by health, for all your character development and enjoyment. Without energy and vitality, you can't do a thing. The physical body acts as a barometer through which our spiritual and mental actions are expressed. So, if our body is 'out of sync' it will have a direct effect on our mental expression and subsequent happiness. The Angel of Health is crucial because she makes us care for our physical body, breathing properly, eating the right foods, getting sufficient rest and relaxation and exercising on a regular basis, all the things that the Assassins would have you relinquish.

Character Assassins love feeding on your energy. Remember the times when you felt low, depressed or unhappy, how much energy did you have? Enough for a three-mile run, or a three-hour snooze? Personally, I got so lethargic I could barely make it through the day. A sedentary lifestyle with my bottom firmly welded to my office chair, busy accumulating executive wadding, was a suicidal way for me to live. Given a horizontal surface and five minutes, I could drop off to sleep anytime, any place, anywhere.

The human body is the best picture of the human soul

Feeling depleted of energy is very common. Our bodies only have so much energy at their disposal, and if we squander this on our emotional life, then we will become physically as well as mentally bankrupt.

As I see it, every day you can do one of two things: build health or produce disease in yourself. If people say to me, 'I haven't got time to exercise, I haven't got time to eat or relax properly', then I say 'You haven't got time not to'. Since none of us can guarantee radiant health for the rest of our lives, we might as well slow up the process of decay.

Four Simple Steps Towards Health and Happiness

If you can master the basics of health, your self-esteem will go through the roof. Forget all of those complex techniques, programmes and plans, just get the basics right: Breathe, Eat, Move and Relax.

Step 1. Breathe

Being unhappy is incredibly draining. One of the reasons for this is because during periods of stress we are more preoccupied with emotional thoughts than with breathing technique. Your energy goes to your head instead of your lungs, making you feel tired and lethargic.

If we learn to breathe properly, it can change the way we feel in body and mind: it can calm us, take away the sick, tight stomach of fear, accelerate our energy and give us a deep, drugless sleep every night.

Breathing can also have an effect on medical conditions: it can lower the

Being unhappy is incredibly draining.

heart and metabolic rate, normalise blood pressure and decrease the cardio-vascular risk, all for free and all by yourself. And it only takes a little practice to learn to breathe correctly.

How Are You Breathing?

You may well think your breathing technique is just fine already. However it probably isn't. While we are growing up, we acquire poor breathing habits, instead of breathing deeply, i.e. taking big hefty snorfling jobs, we tone down our breathing capacity to shallow little sniffles, very dainty, but hopelessly inefficient.

Just by improving your capacity for breathing you can increase your levels of energy and health. At the moment, I bet most of you breathe only into the upper lungs, taking in about the equivalent of a tumbler full of air, but we can actually take in four times more than that.

So How Do We Begin to Breathe Properly?

Start with long, deep diaphragmatic breaths. By learning to breathe more deeply, you can pace yourself when you get tense and irritated. You become in control of yourself.

1. **Find somewhere to sit, keeping your spine straight.**

2. **Relax your shoulders and your chest.**

3. **Breathe in! Think of it as pouring water into a glass from the top and it fills from the bottom. Air comes in through your nose but you are going to fill your abdomen first. Put your hand on your tummy and feel the air filling the space.**

4. **Hold your breath for as long as you feel comfortable (if you go scarlet, keel over and stop breathing altogether, it's a fair indication that you've held your breath for too long).**

5. **When you've filled your lungs, start expelling the air right from the bottom again. Take twice as long as you took to inhale. You can breathe through your mouth if you want.**

6. **Take ten of these breaths four times a day.**

Once you can get into the habit of breathing like this, you can do it anywhere. The supermarket queue, on the escalators in the underground, or at your desk.

Go on. Before you read the next bit take a swig from the oxygen bar and down ten deep breaths.

Step 2. Eat

Good nutrition is crucial for self-care, health and happiness.

There's a hell of a lot of confusion when it comes to what constitutes a well-balanced, healthy diet. What is clear is that food, as a fuel, is an essential source of energy for our bodies to function. As I've already said, feeling down about yourself can sap you of energy, and if you're hungry too you can become even more cranky and negative; eating healthy food can help you maintain a positive attitude towards life. So if you are feeling depleted of energy, or depressed and you are currently on a diet, get off it now!

OK, So What Do We Eat?

There are so many diets, all of them claiming health benefits, longevity and high-energy perks, that it becomes difficult to assess what is what.

In the 80s, it was the F-plan which resulted in your friends spending their time backing away from you, with their handbags over their noses. The 90s is all about combining the different food groups in the right way to aid digestion. Nutrition can be a highly confusing business so just use your common sense as far as possible.

Rules for Healthy Eating

- ❤ Out with the processed rubbish and in with the fresh stuff, organic if possible.

- ❤ Eat if your body wants you to, give yourself permission to eat.

- ❤ Don't trust food advertising.

- ❤ Legalise all foods without feeling guilty.

- ❤ Eat small meals every three to five hours. Eat less to live longer.

- ❤ Don't count calories.

- ❤ Take a sledgehammer to the bathroom scales.

- ❤ Eat in a relaxed environment, sitting down and taking time to chew and enjoy your food.

- ❤ Drink more water.

- ❤ Cut down on fats.

- ❤ Don't add salt.

- ❤ Take nutritional supplements.

- ❤ Vary food so you don't get bored.

- ❤ Don't drink too much fizzy pop.

- ❤ Notice how your body reacts to certain foods.

- ❤ Don't stick grapes up your nose.

Take a sledgehammer
to the bathroom scales.

In short, be sensible but enjoy your food. On the whole, we are educated enough to recognise what has 'coronary' stamped all over it and what types of food we should eat, i.e. fruit and fibre, etc. Many women are veggie which is great and thankfully a far cry from the uncompromising diet of older generations. For example, people like my father who won't touch vegetarian food unless the cook's holding a shotgun to his head!

There are tons of books out there which explain the principles of high energy diets much better than I can. Buy one and learn. You are all highly intelligent beings, so invest in yourself, and reap the rewards.

Step 3. Move

Apart from controlling your breathing, the other way to get more oxygen into your body naturally is through exercise. A simple concept, but one the majority of us hardly relishes.

If you're anything like me, you probably hated doing sports at school - cross-country runs in nipple-hardening weather, wearing shape-challenged

> *Health is the vital principle of bliss,*
> *and exercise of health*

PT shorts killed my Olympic spirit somewhat. With such vivid memories, later in my life the thought of any form of exercise would immediately unleash an elaborate avoidance strategy.

The problem was, that by opting to become a sedentary slug, I was unwittingly ripping myself off. Women who don't exercise are often less healthy, less confident and don't like themselves as much as women who do. Energy creates energy while doing nothing just makes you tired and when you are tired, it's very difficult to be motivated, make plans, reach goals or change.

All in all not much of a life.

So if you want a life you must move. Not only does regular exercise boost our energy levels, it also has massive stress-busting abilities as it gets the blood circulating and feeds the muscles that are badly affected by stress. This is because we carry our suppressed emotions around with us - in our muscle clusters, such as the neck and the shoulders. Exercise also straightens your posture, strength and stamina, burns fat, improves your digestion and breathing, gives you a healthier blood cholesterol level, lowers blood pressure, strengthens bones, decreases the likelihood of a heart attack and generally helps to prolong life. **SOME PANACEA!**

The ultimate magic about exercise is that it makes you feel better about yourself. It raises your self-esteem and gives you buckets of confidence. And it doesn't matter if you're a size eight or size twenty-eight. If you exercise regularly and you are fit, you will like yourself more, regardless of your weight and shape.

Exercise doesn't need to control your life, nor to involve too much effort.

WARNING!

George Dennison Prentice:

What some call health, if purchased by perceptual anxiety about diet, isn't much better than tedious disease.

Let's get one thing absolutely straight. Being healthy and fit is not about being obsessive about your body and the way that you look. Overdoing it can be as harmful as doing no exercise at all. Don't confuse over-dieting and over-exercising with being healthy. It is not. In fact the reverse is true; it is highly dangerous. Becoming over-concerned with what you eat and how much you exercise can make you excessively boring and rigid. In the worst cases, it can wreak havoc on your life through anorexia, bulimia and other obsessive disorders.

Be sensible about exercise and diet and make sure that you have a balanced approach to your health.

So How Much is Enough ?

If you always start fitness programmes with the best intentions, but never last very long, maybe you've been aiming too high or doing a type of exercise which doesn't suit you.

All that's necessary is that we boost our energy levels in some kind of aerobic activity, performed for 30 minutes at least three times a week, preferably most days. Work your way up slowly to some kind of aerobic activity until you can go for 30 minutes without pain or stress.

Do Exercise that is Tailor-made for You

Failing at school sports can put people off sport for life. On top of this the thought of bouncing around doing aerobics in a room full of intimidating women sporting lurid thongs and clenching their buttocks to the latest cardio-funk routine, can also be most off-putting. And yet none of these things need leave you feeling like a reject in the world of fitness.

Here's the good news, you don't have to do aerobics or go to the gym or anything else like that in order to stay fit.

People are intrinsically different. Our genetic make-up is expressed by our individual body type. Different physical types will respond to, enjoy and benefit from different types of sports and exercise. So if you hate hockey and have a complete aversion to aerobics, perhaps they are just the wrong sports for you.

Finding the right type exercise for you really to enjoy won't happen straight away. Try out a few types to see what you like best. It's then only a matter of time before you find a regime that suits you and that you really enjoy.

Here are a few ideas:

♥ *Slow and Calming Exercise*

Tai chi, yoga, martial arts, swimming, horse-riding, walking, touring,
low-impact aerobics, bicycle touring, sailing, diving.

♥ *Fast and Frenzied Exercise*

Aerobics, cross-country running, volleyball, rock-climbing, wild and abandoned sex, dancing (e.g. Latino or Belly Dancing) water-skiing, basketball, tap, ice-skating, snow-skiing, tennis, badminton.

♥ *Fun Exercise*

Things you do with your friends and family or the dog. Walks in the park, going to discos, sex, trampolining, roller-blading, shopping, if you take it seriously (trying clothes on can be exhausting!).

❤ *Stuff Exercise*   Housework, gardening, chasing after kids, walking up the stairs, answering the door, taking out the rubbish. This is where we expend much of our energy.

❤ *Pretend Exercise*   Toning tables, where you lie on a bed that jiggles you around. Having those little electrical paddy things stuck on your wobbly bits in a vain attempt to firm them up. Having an aerobics party where you open a bottle of vino, then spend the rest of the evening slagging off the leotards.
(NB: None of these things really help tax your cardio-vascular system.)

The secret is to find something you really love doing because you will then exercise for longer. But you must start moving now.

PS: Don't look too closely here. I do exercise but I'm not *Gladiator* material. If they wanted me, I'd be called Fluffy.

Step 4. Relax

The 90s was supposed to be the decade where we finally got to put our feet up, do hobbies, poodle around in a less hectic manner and just generally chill out. No such luck I'm afraid. In fact stress, especially at work, has turned into the 90's plague. More often than not stress is worse for women because we may have to juggle two roles, that of a caring mother, while at the same time functioning as a businesswoman.

Apart from the moving breathing and eating, we have to learn to relax if we want to avoid the inevitable burnout that stress can bring. This means slowing down and taking things a whole lot easier if we are to stay in good health.

Leonardo da Vinci:

Every now and then go away, and have a little relaxation,
for when you come back to your work your judgement
will be surer; since to remain constantly at work
will cause you to lose power of judgement . . .
Go some distance away because the work seems smaller
and more of it can be taken in at a glance, and a lack of
harmony or proportion is more readily seen.

Relaxation must be mental and physical. You can learn to relax through progressive muscle relaxation, meditation or yoga. These will reduce tension and improve sleep. You don't have to be a seeker in search of enlightenment or a freak hooked on cosmic experiences in order to do yoga, meditate or start diffusing aromatherapy oils up your nostrils. No way! This stuff is for everybody.

Four Ways to Get Off the Wheel

1 *Yoga* Exercises the muscles and stimulates the breathing, as well as influencing the hormones. Yoga is great because it works the whole spectrum of the mind and body simultaneously whereas Western techniques focus on the body and mind separately.

2 *Go Herbal* You can buy herbs from any health food shop or a direct marketing source. Herbs for relaxation include camomile, which is good for the digestive system, and rosemary for calming yourself before an important meeting. Passionflower aids sleep, limeflower is helpful for a mood verging on angry hysteria, while lemon balm helps restore balance to anxious, depressive states.

3 *Meditate* In the USA meditators get a discount on their health insurance, with good reason. Research has shown that when comparing businessmen the ones that meditated spent much less time in hospital, had 87% fewer benign and malignant tumours, 55% fewer mental disorders and 30% fewer infectious diseases. Meditation works because you are focusing your mind on one thing and not thinking about ten different things at once. Tina Turner insists that it was meditation that helped her build up her confidence again after the break up with her abusive husband Ike. Other meditators include Diana Ross, Demi Moore, Stephanie Beacham and Sandie Shaw. If you can't quite manage meditation then sitting quietly listening to some music could have similar benefits.

4 *Pamper Yourself* Go on lots of short trips, relax in long hot baths with oils, have massages and facials, read a book or even just spend an evening messing around with your hair, so long as it quietens your overactive mind.

THE BIG BOTTOM LINE

How much longer can you afford to let your energy sleep? Doing battle with the Assassins in the short term can be an enormous drain on your energy so you need to make sure you have plenty of it. Breathe, eat and move well, while taking time to relax if you really want to feel alive again.

Guardian Angel 4:
COMPETENCE

When Ffyona Campbell arrived in John O'Groats at the age of 27 she entered the history books as the first woman to have completed an around-the-world walk. Only three people went before her, all of them men. It had taken Ffyona 11 years to cover the 17,000 plus miles travelling across four continents and encountering, along the way, tests of physical and mental endurance beyond most of our imaginations. However, on the very first day of her mammoth trek, she whispered to herself, *'Don't be frightened, you're just going for a walk.'*

Doubtless there were many occasions when she thought of quitting but those moments were powerless when subjected to Ffyona's stubborn determination and overpowering self-belief. Reflecting on those low days she said, 'The lowest you can get is when you stop believing in yourself, and I've almost been there quite a few times. . . but I never did hit rock bottom, and that's why I'm here today' *(The Catalyst Magazine)*.

The reasons why Ffyona embarked on this mercurial walking expedition are best known to herself, but she has become an icon, a source of inspiration, a symbol of what women could achieve and a role model of possibility.

> ## *Whether you think you can or you can't, you're right*

As humans we are driven to achieve because we need to feel a sense of competence; the ability to carry out an intended action satisfactorily. It earns us our self-respect and the respect of others. If we feel competent, we believe we can make things happen for ourselves in the world. Something that is crucial to self-esteem.

Our sense of competence is challenged throughout our lives. Some people feel capable of dealing with anything, others feel out of their depth. Character Assassins such as Negative Self-Belief and Foolish Expectations attack Competence. The question is, does Competence come out the victor, or is she assassinated, so that you feel unable to rise to certain challenges in life?

How competent we feel can usually be traced back to something in our past: from family, peers and teachers. Usually it remains buried in our subconscious, emerging years later as a Character Assassin such as the 'Inner Bitch'. Before you try anything she tells you in no uncertain terms that 'You're going to fail, flunky face'. And if on the off-chance you succeed, she's even more poisonous: 'Huh! Well, that was dead easy anyway, a Sesame Street audience could have done that'. What a cow!

Of course you are always going to encounter the tribe know as doubters throughout your life. My advice is to listen to Ffyona Campbell who spouted this genius piece of metaphysical wisdom on completing her world wide walk . . .

'Don't let the b***** get you down!'**

Levels of Competence are not Measured by IQ

Learning to feel more competent and in control of our lives involves putting to bed some very prevalent myths. The first is the notion that competence is measured by your ability to do algebra, the Times crossword or argue the merits of the ERM membership. This vision of competence infers that formal education is the true measure of character and self-fulfilment. It encourages a kind of intellectual snobbery which has completely obscured the true meaning of competence.

> *The reason most people flounder is not through lack of education but a lack of goals*

Such methods of assessing competence could not be further from the truth.

Research has shown that, as individuals, we each have a preferred way of receiving information, either through sight, sound or feeling. Psychologists refer to these 'pathways' as Visual, Auditory and Kinesthetic. A visual child will learn best through the use of diagrams, an auditory child through spoken words and a kinesthetic child will benefit most from practical examples. In many cases, a child's difficulties in grasping a subject will be the result of the way in which it is being taught. If a teacher draws diagrams on the blackboard, it could be a real struggle for a non-visual child to grasp the information.

So let me tell you something right now! If you had difficulties learning in school and the other kids seemed to learn faster, it was probably because you had a different learning strategy, not that you were stupid or incompetent.

If you want to feel competent then simply look at the things you've done which have boosted your self-esteem. The things that have given you a sense of achievement. And your achievements can be absolutely anything: keeping house, bringing up children, playing the piano, yoga, singing, cooking, reading, a career, sport, whatever.

All of us are born with the capacity to feel competent in life. We just need to realise it.

How Can I Start to Feel Competent and have a Sense of Achievement?

Just relax for a second and imagine you are at the opening of a new art gallery. You're there on your own, having a sneak preview of a brilliant new exhibition dedicated to **your achievements.** On display are images depicting times from your past when you've been at your very best or done some-

A brilliant new exhibition.

thing well. As you wander around, gaze at the murals, paintings and photographs, images of those special moments will remind you that you can achieve, that you have experienced happiness in the past and of course that you will do so in the future.

These images from your past could be anything from throwing a successful dinner party, getting engaged, getting divorced(!), having a baby, travelling to a foreign country, being healthy, achieving some balance in your life, resolving a conflict at work, getting a promotion and taking risks during negotiations. List anything at all that may have boosted your self-esteem.

One last request. While you're looking at all your past achievements, lift your right hand to just above your left shoulder. Start motioning with the hand in an up and down repetitive fashion, lightly hitting the back of your shoulder. Well done. You have just given yourself something that is rarely self-administered . . . a 'pat on the back'.

Give yourself a pat on the back

Do this as regularly as possible, because the quality of your life depends on it.

The Secrets of Consistent Achievement

Helen Hayes:

My mother drew a distinction between achievement and success. She said that achievement is the knowledge that you have studied and worked hard and done the best that is in you. Success is being praised by others, and that's nice too, but not as important or satisfying.
Always aim for achievement and forget about success.

The purpose of life is not to be successful. Or rather it is, but not according to the definition of success that most people seem to use. The idea is not to become better than anyone else, or be more famous, rich and respected, but just be the best you can be.

To do this, try the following:

1. Set Achievable Goals that Stretch You

In five years' time you are going to arrive somewhere, but the question is where? We can't go through life with our fingers crossed; the future doesn't get better through hope or visiting tarot card readers.

> ## *A person going nowhere can be sure of reaching her destination*

Quite simply your life can't go according to plan when you don't have a plan, and this means having goals. If you think you'll achieve all you want to without clearly defined and written goals then you are labouring under an illusion, in fact you'll probably have more success trying to pin blancmange to a wall.

If you can set a goal properly then you are halfway to reaching it. Let me show you how to do it.

You'll probably have more success trying to pin blancmange to a wall.

1. Create a wish list.

Go crazy and write down all the things that you ever wanted to achieve in life. All the things you want to be, to have and to do. (Write it in code if it's too pornographic.) Sit down right now, grab a pen and start writing. Don't worry about the <u>how</u>, just write the <u>what</u>. Remember: there are no limits!

2. Look over your wish list,

estimating when you expect to achieve these outcomes. One month? One year? Ten years? You have to commit yourself to a time-frame or else your goals will remain fanciful wishes.

3. Now pick four goals that you can achieve this year.

Pick out the goals that you are most committed to, most excited about and that will give you the most satisfaction. Rewrite them, chop them down into bite-size chunks and state the reasons why you will achieve them.

Remember: There are no limits!

4. Describe the kind of person you would have to be to attain your goals.

Will you have more courage, self-discipline or responsibility? Do you need to go on a course to learn new skills or change job? What would you need to be successful?

Re-read everything you've written and think for a while. Create a mental picture of yourself achieving the things you've always wanted. How will that make you feel?

Transfer all this information to a journal that you can refer to easily. Every week re-read and modify them if necessary, or tear them up and start again. Goal setting is not something that you do just once, it's a continual process.

Some Useful Tips

❤ When you set your goals, be as specific as possible using a set of concisely worded phrases which paint a detailed picture of the 'better you' or the change in your life you would like to create. By doing this in advance, you provide an inspiration to keep moving towards that vision.

💙 Write down your goals in the present tense, using affirmations as though they'd already been achieved. For example, 'I have now set up my own publishing company and published two magazines'; 'I have left my job and am having an unbelievable time travelling around the world covering over 32 countries'; 'I now have a fabulous house in the country, a husband and two beautiful children'.

💙 When you accomplish a goal, give yourself a TREAT, preferably one that's good for you! For example Mississippi Mud Pie (choccy cake with steroids) is not the ideal treat to celebrate losing 2lb in weight!

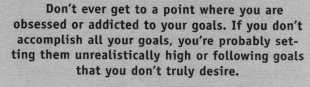

WARNING!

Don't ever get to a point where you are obsessed or addicted to your goals. If you don't accomplish all your goals, you're probably setting them unrealistically high or following goals that you don't truly desire.

DON'T TAKE ON TOO MUCH AT ONCE.

If you're finding it really hard to sit down and visualise your goals, don't worry. Avoidance and trivial distractions are normal feelings that precede the process.
If you don't accomplish a goal, don't assume that you have failed. Simply acknowledge that you have not accomplished that goal and decide whether you want to set it again or let it go. Otherwise you may feel that you have failed.

2. Be Persistent

'Slow and steady wins the race', says Aesop in his familiar fable of the tortoise and the hare. Long term progress is sometimes hard to see in the short term; that's why, when it comes to achieving your goals, you need <u>continual</u>, <u>sustained</u> and <u>unremitting</u> **ACTION**. In others words, **persistence**.

> *No-one is ever whipped until they quit, in their own mind*

If you don't stick at things in life, or you hesitate and procrastinate there's a strong chance that you might fail. On the other hand, if you choose to develop persistence, then you are able to sweep aside the obstacles that stand between you and your goals. Your persistence then develops into a respected and proven progressive power.

Calvin Coolidge:

> Nothing in the world can take the place of persistence.
> Talent will not: nothing is more common than unsuccessful
> women with talent. Genius will not; unrewarded genius is
> almost a proverb. Education will not; the world is full of
> educated derelicts. Persistence and determination
> alone are omnipotent.

There are many stories of how women persisted against the odds to achieve what they wanted to. And it's never too late, I read recently about a lady who for years lived in the lavatories in Piccadilly underground station, living a life of misery, punctuated by drink and drugs, violence, prostitution and prison. But in her mid-fifties and at an all-time low she decided to turn her life around and embark on an educational adventure which took eight years to complete. The result was a Master's degree in English from Oxford University.

Never! Never! Never! Never! Give up!

Her ambition is to become a doctor by the turn of the century and she will do it. Her persistence has brought about an astonishing triumph late in life, long beyond the age that most women think about achieving their ambition. Her story proves a triumph for the human spirit and a burning desire to feel competent.

Whatever you do, don't give up, hang in there. The painting is not dry yet, see yourself as an undiscovered masterpiece with a million things left to learn about yourself.

See yourself as an undiscovered masterpiece.

Note: Triumph is made up of two words. **TRY** and **UMPH.** Trying comes from persisting and the Umph is what you get from . . .

3. Passion

Finally, the real trigger for all achievement is passion. A hot, steamy, sweaty Passion. To commit yourself absolutely to your goals, you need to have a burning desire for them. Why else should you put yourself through the pain?

Unleash your passion!

THE BIG BOTTOM LINE

To feel success in some achievement which you regard as your own thing, is vital to self-esteem. Instead of setting goals based on results, set goals which focus on performance.

Happiness lies in the joy of achievement, the thrill of creative effort and the resulting feelings of competence.

Guardian Angel 5:
Sense of Purpose

As a producer of some of Britain's most popular television shows, Sarah Jarman had everything going for her: a middle-class background, a comfortable London flat, rubbing shoulders with celebrities and an enviable choice of work offers.

But in 1987 the £50 000-a-year media executive began to question what she was doing with her life. She started a mission which took her to the dangerous streets of Brazil, trying to save some of the world's poorest children from drugs, prostitution, gang warfare and police death squads.

Sarah now lives in Brazil where she looks after thirty street urchins at a time. Every day a team from her Happy Child Mission tours the city streets helping youngsters at risk. Looking back on her former lifestyle, 35-year-old Sarah says:

I think if I had stayed in television I would have done very well, I was offered some great shows. It's a tough, nasty business but I was very ambitious. But I never look back and wonder if I've done the right thing. What I am doing today is the biggest production I've ever worked on, seeing lives being transformed.

Daily Mail 5 June 1996

Since the beginning of time, mankind has attempted to discover the meaning of life. Our pilgrimage to the City of Happiness in some respects is nothing more than a crusade for a cause bigger than our own lives. As Plato remarked *'Our Purpose is to realise our potential'*. We are given life and our purpose is to make a success of it in terms of what we give back to the world, becoming fulfilled ourselves in the process. Deep within all of us there is a Purposeful Angel who loves to defend justice and support those who are less fortunate than ourselves.

Meanwhile, back at the City of Doom, the Character Assassins are working frenetically to condition you not to recognise your purpose by placing limitations on your life. Purpose is anathema to them, so to counter this the Assassins do their best to instill feelings of being useless, ineffectual, non-functioning, pointless, directionless . . . in a nutshell downright purposelessness. Bless their nylon socks.

The psychologist and philosopher **Carl Jung** wrote,

The Character Assassins will try to stop you from reaching your purpose.

'About a third of my cases are not suffering from any clinically definable neuroses, but from the senselessness and aimlessness of their lives. Feeling futile and having a lack of purpose just breeds disease and disharmony.'

When you have Purpose in life you find that you become totally overwhelmed with a reason for living. This then gives you a deep certainty, clarity, energy, vision and strength. Purpose is a fundamental human need: until you connect your life to a Purpose then your life will have little meaning.

The Austrian psychiatrist, **Dr Victor E Frankl**, survived years of torture in Nazi concentration camps. While he was there he studied the motivations behind why some people survived and others didn't. He was fascinated that many strong young men and women would die in months whilst weaker, older people lived for years. Stripped of all external props, he found that only those with a <u>reason</u> to live, survived. His horrific experiences taught him that a man or woman can survive any hardship so long as his or her *meaning of life* remains intact.

After the war, Dr Frankl founded the school of psychology called logotherapy, based on the Greek word logos which means 'meaning'. In his book, *Man's Search for Meaning,* he wrote:

Man's search for meaning is the primary motivation in his life and not a secondary rationalisation of instinctual drives. This meaning is unique and specific in that it must and can be fulfilled by him alone; only then does it achieve a significance which will satisfy his own will to meaning.

What Exactly is Purpose?

In today's changing times, everyone needs a meaning in life, or Purpose, more than ever. So what exactly is it?

Your Purpose is much more than goals: Goals are just stepping stones toward your Purpose. Perfecting the ultimate soufflé or having a stomach like a washboard are not Purposes, but they may be goals. Goals are essential, though, because they allow you to realise your Purpose and help you affirm that you are going in the right direction. It is therefore important that your goals are in line with your Purpose in life.

Nearly all Purposes are about service to others: We are in the world to change it for the better. Your Purpose does not have to be charity-based but it should be based on positively affecting people. For example, a great purpose could be 'To make as many people as possible laugh through my natural wit'. Once you find your purpose in life all I can say is that helping others just gets to you in ways that you can't anticipate. You find true joy and happiness in life when you give and give and go on giving and never count the cost. The effect it has on your self-esteem is incredible. By leaving a legacy, you will find meaning in living, loving and learning.

Purpose is a catalyst: It helps you push through all the pain necessary to achieve your goal. But you also need a Purpose if you really want to experience **PASSION.**

Ordinary people do extraordinary things because they are totally driven by passion. **Mother Teresa** of Calcutta voluntarily suffers for a humanitarian cause, enduring working conditions that for most of us would be intolerable, to help the poverty-stricken and sick in the name of God. She suffers to achieve a Purpose that is meaningful to her. There is no secret formula to her incredible life, she is simply following her mission.

How to Find Your Purpose

We were all put here for a very specific reason, it's not, 'she who dies with the most Versace outfits, wins'. It's about 'what is ultimately important to you as a person'. You need to do some soul searching. What legacy do you want to leave from your life?

> **Many persons have a wrong idea of what constitutes true happiness. It is not attained through self gratification but through fidelity to a worthy purpose**

Discovering what you want in life is actually quite straightforward, all you do is study your dreams. What's your real passion? What really gets the hairs on the back of your neck bristling? What would you like to do more than anything else? Teach people, make others laugh, assist the disadvantaged, lead people, develop natural resources?

Just dare to imagine the future you would like to live, like these women did:

Sally Gunnell	British Olympic Hurdling Champion
Dame Kiri Te Kanawa	One of the world's greatest female opera singers
Margaret Thatcher	Prime Minister
Evelyn Glennie	Top musician
Anita Roddick	Owner of the Body Shop
Whitney Houston	international singing megastar
Martina Navratilova	Umpteen times Wimbledon Tennis Champion
Julia Roberts	One of Hollywood's highest-paid actresses
Mother Teresa	Nobel peace prize winner
Oprah Winfrey	The highest-paid talk show host in the world
Liz McColgan	British Long-Distance Olympic Champion

Is there anything these women have that you don't? **ABSOLUTELY NOTHING!** Most of them came from very ordinary, even disadvantaged, backgrounds. The only distinguishing feature is that they have had a burning ambition and the courage to follow it. Great people are just ordinary people with great determination.

> ## *The future belongs to those who believe in the beauty of their dreams*

I guarantee that the whole time these women were trying to move towards their purpose, their Character Assassins sat there roaring like lions. Fortunately, they made damn sure that they didn't succumb.

Now of course, I am not asking you to do what these women did; your purpose may be totally different. Variety is what makes life so interesting. However, what you can do is mirror their achievements.

Sharon Stone (*Daily Mail* 27 May 1995):

> When I was a kid growing up in Meadville, Pennsylvania, I said I was going to be an actress and everyone told me I was crazy. It took me 13 years before I had a hit movie. It took a lot of willpower and fortitude to keep working towards my dreams.

When I gave up work (a frightening prospect) it wasn't because I couldn't bear the thought of another day of nylons, office politics and undrinkable MaxPax coffee. I simply looked at my life and thought 'OK, I'm successful at what I do, but I'm not pursuing my heart's desire'. It was seriously affecting my self-esteem and my brain was beginning to fry.

Then I asked myself, what did I really want to do? The thing that

My brain was beginning to fry.

really got me excited was a dream to research and teach character development. . . maybe even write a book. This is where my true direction lay.

Leaving my job heralded a radical departure in my life. On top of this I had little money, little security, no previous experience of this subject, no publishing deal, heaps of criticism and zippo support. I had met my Waterloo.

Frankly I was scared stiff.

But this was what I wanted, damn it! And guess what, it's amazing how easily, once you commit yourself, things happen. Suddenly the world makes way for the woman who knows where she's going. Life is funny like that, it has a way of hiding all the answers and revealing them to the people who are inspired to look for them.

WARNING !

The majority of people who don't have a purpose in life don't bother to go and look for it. They think that their purpose is the sort of thing that only reveals itself when it's good and ready. Wrong. Don't fall into the trap of just waiting for that flash of inspiration to tell you what your life is all about; go and look for it.

Don't wait for your ship to come in; swim out to it.

Although you may be completely clueless about what you feel your purpose is in life, don't worry. Even as you sit there reading this book your subconscious is desperately tapping on the window of your conscious mind trying to get through via your dreams, intuition and innermost longings. To speed up the process of finding your purpose you first have to plant the seed. Do this by asking yourself some questions.

Three Questions that will Bring You Closer to Your Purpose

Write down your answers to the following questions over and over again. Sooner or later, by just keeping the questions in the forefront of your mind and reviewing the answers, you will get to the point where you are able to define your true Purpose in life.

1 - if i didn't have to work for a living, what would i love to do most?

2 - if i won ten million pounds tax free on the Lottery, what would i do? (After paying bills and buying luxuries!)

3 - if i found out that i only had six months of healthy life to live, what would i do right now? (What would i want to leave as a legacy?)

Just list anything that comes into your mind, don't prejudge anything. Then ask 'What's important about me doing that?' Keep plonking the ideas down until you get to the essence of what is really important to you, don't forget, this takes time!

When finally you realise what your life's Purpose is, without wanting to sound too schmaltzy, 'it will touch your heart'. There is something you can do that will make a difference. You don't have to become the next Margaret Thatcher or Mother Teresa, just do whatever you can do to fulfil your Purpose. It doesn't matter if you are recognised for your actions or not, you will know when you have achieved them.

Eleanor Roosevelt:

When you cease to make a contribution, you begin to die.

THE BIG BOTTOM LINE

Your Purpose is the most important thing in life. If you don't have Purpose in place then all your actions will be empty and misdirected.

Guardian Angel 6: Sense of Identity

Bette Midler:

Cherish forever what makes you unique, cuz you're really a yawn if it goes!

To know who you are is perhaps the most important and least recognised need of the human soul. 'Who am I?' 'What am I?' 'How do I define me?' Everything you think, judge, feel, value, honour, esteem, love, hate, fear, desire, hope for, believe in and are committed to, combine to create the unique You. All these criteria define you as a person, and they are constantly in the process of change. You are unique, one of a kind, a perfect specimen of **You.**

> *Learning to love yourself is the greatest love of all.*

We need this knowledge of who we are, independent of other people because it engenders within us a **strong sense of identity.** When you are able to identify who you are, you achieve a more assertive character (without being aggressive) which is essential for self-esteem and happiness.

Unfortunately, though, many women allow the Character Assassins to get to them and as a result end up on the Missing Persons list. They may well be the most important person in the lives of their husband and children, but outside the role of a mother and a housewife they feel like a big Zero. Feeling like a nobody, unable to comprehend that they are important, special and highly capable human beings.

Unless you feel you are acting, feeling and are recognised in a way that reflects the real you, you leave yourself wide open to those deadly Character Assassins – They are sure to prey on your weakness.

How We Start to Lose Our Identity

Amanda de Cadenet:

> One big thing I have a problem with is that so much of my
> identity is hung on the people I know.

The problem is that many of us have lost the knowledge about who we are because society teaches us to conform, to be just another boring little ant on the anthill. So instead of being true to who we really are, we start to fake our beliefs and values in order that we may FIT IN. By misrepresenting our reality by pretending to be somebody that we are not, we are deceiving ourselves.

To be different is a wonderful thing

**To be different is a
wonderful thing.**

But They Might not Like who I Am!

I am afraid to tell you who I am because if I do, you might not like who I am and it's all I have. . . Isn't that how it goes?

So why are we so afraid that people might not like who we really are? None of us wants to be a fraud or live a lie but many of us are terrified of **REJECTION.** Since Eve wore her snakeskin miniskirts to pull Adam, the fear of rejection remains a highly emotive issue because we crave love and acceptance. The fear of what honest expression might cause sometimes seem so risky that we take refuge in false roles and disguises.

Our fear about what other people think about us inevitably gears us towards their wants and expectations, and the more we live to meet the expectations of others the more weak and insecure we become. Result - we unwittingly develop a front as thick and rubbery as a frogman's wetsuit.

With no sense of who we are the Assassins move in to manipulate what we feel, say and do. Invariably, we end up doing stupid, **STUPID** things like:

- ❤ **telling people we love them when we don't;**

- ❤ **say we are angry when we are afraid;**

- ❤ **pretending to be helpless when we are actually being manipulative;**

- ❤ **laughing when we actually want to cry;**

- ❤ **denying our excitement about life;**

- ❤ **faking beliefs to win acceptance;**

- ❤ **being kind to everyone except the ones we profess to love;**

- ❤ **spending unnecessary stretches of time with people we don't respect;**

- ❤ **keeping everyone else happy at our expense;**

- ❤ **doing dumb, useless tasks out of fear, guilt, weakness and obligation.**

Cindy Crawford (You Magazine 28 May 1995):

It's really hard when you first meet someone because you want them to like you, so you try to be who they want you to be. Who you are comes out sooner or later anyway.

As we pretend to be someone else we lose our identity and, in the process, we lose touch with our real feelings, needs and desires. We start to depend on external things to create a false identity and act completely out of character. This continuous inconsistency with who we are steers us at alarming speed into an Identity Crisis.

Avoiding an Identity Crisis

When you fall prey to an identity crisis it hits you like a sledgehammer. Suddenly you become disorientated so it becomes impossible to distinguish who you really are at any given moment. If you are not having an identity crisis yet, then here are four easy steps on how to keep avoiding it:

1 Don't try to please all the people all of the time.

2 Don't be a fashion victim.

3 Don't take yourself at face value.

4 Don't let labels obscure your real identity.

1. Don't Try to Please All the People All of the Time

Michelle Collins (Cindy on *Eastenders* on being asked about her Epitaph, *Daily Mail* 8 June 1995):

Do you think they liked me?

I'm a real worrier and sensitive about what impression I make. But in trying to please everyone you can end up upsetting everyone.

Trying to please all the people all of the time is inherent in women, because our ability to get on with others is directly related to our self-esteem. Our programming subtly implies that we must please everybody, because to be universally liked is of paramount importance. So we exhibit an infinite supply of caring towards everybody we meet, giving and giving until it hurts and then giving a little bit more.

Sally Field:

> I was raised to sense what someone wanted me to be and be kind to that person. It took me a long time not to judge myself through someone else's eyes.

In the long run you will discover that by maintaining a false front and becoming all things to all people demands different things of you. If you are true to one person you may have to suddenly let somebody else down by swapping allegiance. But you can't bear the thought of that so in order to please everybody you have to wear masks, play games and put on appearances to get by. This huge effort to keep the entire world happy soon blows up in your face as you inevitably get found out and people start to see you as flaky, fickle, unreliable and untrustworthy. The result: apart from compromising your identity you also lose the respect of others.

Fiona Fullerton (*Daily Mail*, 26 September 1994):

> After my nervous breakdown for which I had to be hospitalised, I took a long hard look at myself, and didn't like what I saw. A long standing on-off relationship which was making me miserable, my acting career was in the doldrums and my sexy party girl image was doing me no favours. In the past I was so confused. I wore low-cut dresses because I thought that was what men wanted. But actually I was frightening off the nice ones with my sexy glamorous image. A lot of men just saw me as a trophy.

By keeping everything and everybody else happy you are continually living an act and living falsely. You are unaware of what you really need or want. However, none of this confusion and heartache occurs if you have a strong sense of identity because you don't allow others' attitudes and behaviour to influence your beliefs about yourself. Instead you judge yourself by your own criteria, feeling secure within your own boundaries without feeling the need to prove anything to anybody. Stop worrying about what others think about you, just say this is **ME**, like it or lump it. Funnily enough, once you get into this settled sense of 'me', then others begin to respond to you in the same way.

This is ME, like it or lump it.

Do what you can to make people happy *so long* as it makes you happy. At the end of the day wouldn't you rather that people responded positively to the real you rather than a false image of you? Anybody who really cares about you wants you to be yourself, anybody who doesn't want that doesn't really care about you. It's as simple as that.

2. Don't be a Fashion Victim

Goldie Hawn:

It took seven years of analysis to discover I could be famous and still be me. I feared I might lose what I liked about myself, the little person who delights in little things, who doesn't need diamonds and furs to be happy. But it made the little me bigger.

In an effort to 'keep up with Joneses' the biggest mistake you can make is to start building your identity through fashion, possessions or status symbols. When you do this you start to live with the belief that only if you 'wear the latest designer outfits', 'lunch at this restaurant', 'belong to this club' or 'live in that district' will you be socially accepted and admired. Life's strategy suddenly revolves around labels and the right addresses as we become convinced that our self-esteem is dependent upon conveying the 'proper' image.

Linda Henley:

. . . So many of us define ourselves by what we have, what we wear, what kind of house we live in and what kind of car we drive. . . If you think of yourself as the woman in the Cartier watch and the Hermes scarf, a house fire will destroy not only your possessions but yourself.

When we identify ourselves and our success or failure by the quantity and quality of our possessions then we are confusing our self-worth as human beings with the acquisition of material objects. What you are really saying is that you alone are not enough. You must continuously replenish your supply of possessions in an effort to feel valued. You

You become your handbag.

become your handbag, your scarf or your watch. . . even if it is a Cartier.

Edwin Hubell Chapin:

> Fashion is a science of appearances, and it inspires one
> with the desire to seem rather than be.

This effort to be 'fashionable' puts you on a treadmill that just gets faster and faster. Ultimately appearances alone will never satisfy. Granted, you may suffer in opulent luxury but you forfeit all sense of identity as long as you remain a slave to objects.

3. Don't Take Yourself at Face Value

Bertolt Brecht:

> People remain what they are, even when
> their faces fall to bits.

If you believe that you are only your body, your looks and your age then prepare to send for the man with the Prozac. It may not have escaped your notice that spots and bad hair days are frequent fixtures in our everyday lives. On top of this, as we get older there is a jolly good chance that we may get wrinkles, grey hair, and saggy bits. These physical changes will cause tremendous suffering if our identity depends on remaining the same as we looked when we were 18 years old, especially when your face starts to resemble a relief map of the Hindu Kush.

By linking our identity with our body as a means of fulfilment we can become obsessed with our appearance. This paranoia is a common breeding ground for the proverbial mid-life crisis, the point at which we try desperately to hold off on the middlescene and swagger along as we did when we were young. To prove we are still young and to maintain our identity we start calling everybody from a divorce lawyer to Vidal Sassoon for a complete makeover, rather than accept the inevitable process

**Spots are fixtures of
our everyday lives**

in a spirit of accommodation and adjustment.

Physical vanity is a compensation for a sense of inferiority as a person. Taken to extremes, these people identify themselves with their bodies; they only think they are good-looking and nothing more.

The more importance we attach to our physical appearance, the less we are able to stand back and see what is truly us. Instead we have a nervous breakdown at the first signs of decay and scupper our chances of learning to relate meaningfully as a person.

I'm not saying *don't* look after your body, quite the reverse. It's just that if we have a strong sense of 'who we are' then gaining a wrinkle, a pound or two or some cellulite, won't have us reaching for the bottle. We are secure about who we are. So just chill out about yourself and stop the fight to maintain that false front, even if it is high-grade plastic, buffered with the finest silicon!

When the character is right the looks are a great delight. This is the true art of beauty.

4. Don't Let Labels Obscure Your Real Identity

Soren Kierkegaard:

> Once you label me you negate me.

Examine the labels that you apply to yourself.

A word of advice: examine the labels that you apply to yourself.

To do this you must refer to your history and the neat little stack of labels you have accumulated over a lifetime. Many of these labels were pinned on you as a child and you carry them around with you to this day. They may include tags like 'I'm nervous', 'I'm shy', 'I'm loving', 'I'm sweet'. Labels are hardly ever applied with sensitivity as to their significance, so although they may be appropriate they can be harmful because every single label has a boundary or a limit of one kind or another.

The very act of labelling may be a specific deterrent to growth. It's easy to use a label to justify maintaining the *status quo*. You can spot a self-limiting label a mile off by the use of neurotic statements such as 'that's me all over', 'I've always been that way' and 'That's my nature'.

Not all labels are bad, but they become so if the label is demeaning or detrimental to your character in some way. People want to pigeon-hole you into neat little categories, it's easier that way. Ironically, nowhere is this more prevalent than in the so-called self-help industry. Here, psycho-labels are reeled out in an attempt to categorise a person as some sort of hapless victim. So instead of being just plain old 'unhappy' with life you are now dysfunctional, co-dependant, narcissistic, hysterical and have an addictive personality.

Some sort of hapless victim?

Kate Millet
(*The Loony Bin Trip*, 1990):

> If only no one had told them I was mad.
> Then I wouldn't be.

Fact: Whatever the conscious mind thinks and believes, the subconscious identically creates. So if someone tells you that you are dysfunctional and you choose to accept this, then guess what? You become defunct and stay that way. The thinking goes like this: if I feel stupid, I am stupid. **FEELING IS BELIEVING.**

Just thank your lucky stars you weren't a mildly depressed woman at the turn of the century, when psychoanalysts such as Freud could pull the seduction theory on you. *Now I vant you to lie on ze couch and relax. I will say a vord and you must say the first vord that comes into your poor distressed mind. Okay?* Before you knew it your general feelings of low self-esteem were put down to overwhelming fantasies of sexual incest. Boy, oh boy, you are von perverted bunny. . . Nice one Sig.

Eliminating the titles and labels allotted to us reduces our inclination to compartmentalise and restrict our lives. View yourself as a human. No labels are necessary.

A Moment of Truth

In order to define who you really are, you need to do a bit of soul searching and honest talking. You may not like every aspect about yourself but likewise, it does not mean denying the reality of who you are. No more cover-ups.

Take a nice deep breath and relax. Now ask, in the privacy of your mind and heart, some questions about yourself. Be curious, not worried or fearful and without looking for perfection. Ask yourself :

Who am I:

- **without my family?**

- **without my popularity?**

- **without my possessions?**

- **without my job?**

- **when there is no one to tell me what to do, no one to obey or impress?**

What is it I hope to win?

What games do I want to play?

What is it I am trying to hide?

Who am I facing in the mirror?

Write down whatever comes in to your mind.

Now take a moment to really appreciate who you are and feel any emotion that comes with the recognition. If this creates pain then instead you can make a list of all the elements of your identity you want to have. Then imagine what you would feel like with these new characteristics and make a plan that will mould you into this new identity. The sooner you accept who you are, then the quicker you may learn what you can become.

By knowing who you are you become more assertive. You will realise that you didn't come to this earth to put yourself out for others in order to be liked, but to allow the spirit inside your body to become free. What others think about you is none of your business, how they react towards you is none of your business. Adopt the attitude 'take me for who I am, or don't take me at all.' One has just to be oneself. That's the Angels' basic message.

The Big Bottom Line

To be yourself, to use your own God-given talent, and to stand up for what is right even in the midst of uncertainty, pain, fear and persecution, is the only true way to live. There is nothing so powerful as the truth. Be what you are. Because this is the real secret to becoming better than you are.

Guardian Angel 7:
ACTIVITY

Charlotte Brontë:

It is vain to say human beings ought to be satisfied with tranquillity: they must have action: and they will make it if they cannot find it.

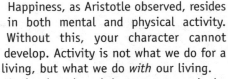

Happiness, as Aristotle observed, resides in both mental and physical activity. Without this, your character cannot develop. Activity is not what we do for a living, but what we do *with* our living.

A developed and happy woman is by nature an active one. She doesn't wait for permission to do things, she just 'gets on with it'. She has no idea how much she weighs or how many blackheads are currently setting up home on her nose. Her motto is 'She who hesitates dies'. If her heart desires, she acts, in spite of any feelings of fear or insecurity that she may have, and lets her subconscious thoughts and feelings run to catch up. 'Wait, you can't do this. You're not up to it', cries the Inner Bitch who ups the ante of insults in order to maintain control: 'You'll make a complete fool of yourself and get hurt'. The busy woman knows how to deal with this. She threatens the Inner Bitch with a vasectomy of the vocal cords. . . the voice that was once loud and so compelling shuts up immediately.

> ### *What you do matters.*
> ### *All you need is to do it.*

The opposite of activity is not leisure, relaxation or enjoyment, but plain idleness. The idle woman is expert at sitting still, the Angel of Activity has completely eluded her, she doesn't 'do' anything and is famed for her limited moving parts. She waits to feel motivated or until fear is looking the

other way before making any sudden movements; for most of the time, she looks as apathetic as a piece of pan-fried cod. In march the Character Assassins, delighted because she can give them 100% of her solid gold, undivided attention. This inevitably wrangles her a one-way ticket back to the City of Doom. *Bon vacances!*

Life is a movable feast. . . but who is moving, it or you?

As apathetic as a piece of pan-fried cod.

You're More than Just a 'Being'!

So many of the self-help gurus today reckon that self-esteem is all about being, not doing. 'To have self-esteem, all you need to do is just feel good about yourself' they say, rather poetically. Great theory, guys, but if you see yourself as an utterly repellent, oversized prune then it's very hard to magic up 'feeling good about yourself' if you haven't 'done' anything to feel good about. I know, because I've tried, and it doesn't work.

> ## *Happiness is found in doing, not merely possessing*

Back in the good old days, before the wacky world of therapy sprang up, 'positive thinking' was an active verb; something that you did as you went about your business. Now self-esteem has been transformed into a condition or syndrome. Social psychologist **Carol Travis** put this development beautifully when she said:

> Self-esteem is now a mere shadow of its former self. Once it referred to a fundamental sense of self-worth, today that meaning has narrowed into merely feeling good about oneself. Self-esteem used to rest on the daily acts of effort, care and accomplishment that are the bedrock of character, now it rests on air, on being instead of doing.

Floating around on a big fluffy cloud of 'being', instead of getting out there and actually 'doing' something, makes it very hard to accept yourself. If you are not 'active', you cannot practice and develop the principles that are crucial to your character.

And so cannot begin to taste the deliciousness of an emerging self-confidence.

Floating around on a big fluffy cloud.

> ## She who isn't busy being born is busy dying

Mere acceptance of who we are simply by 'being' means we negate our power to choose our responses in life. If you don't take a proactive approach and 'do' things, then you become a VVV. . . Victim. Life is too precious and wonderful to stay a victim. So don't just sit down and let life's waters lap around you. . . dive into them.

Activity Has its Own Reward. . . Growth

Abigail Adams:

It is not in the still calm of life, or the repose of a pacific station, that great characters are formed. . . The habits of a vigorous mind are formed in contending with difficulties. All history will convince you of this, and that wisdom and penetration are the fruit of experience, not the lessons of retirement and leisure. Great necessities call out great virtues.

Growth is the only evidence of life. If we don't do things, we don't experience things. If we don't experience, then we don't grow. If we don't grow, we are not really living. It's that simple.

Women who fulfil their need to grow have, in general, given themselves the chance to try new experiences: unfortunately most adults muffle themselves into a cocoon of middle-aged habit and convention by the time they are 25, let alone 45!

By being active we fulfil the need to have experiences and challenges so that we can grow, develop and be alive.

> ## *Knowledge is what you know. Wisdom is what you do with what you know*

Make Sure You Vary Your Activities

Dorothy Parker:

> Listen, Fred, don't feel badly
> when I die, because
> I've been dead for a long time.

Question: When does activity become a life-threatening illness?

Answer: When your activities become so routine and mundane that you die of boredom, from the neck upwards.

We are a restless bunch of individuals and hanker for human experience. If we don't look out, everyday activity, no matter how absorbing, can become too repetitive, too organised and too humdrum.

Depriving ourselves of variety in life is a bit like a hunger for sex. The longer it's left unsatisfied, the more it

Nothing is more dangerous than an activity when it's the only one you have

grows. When all hope of satisfaction fades away, the hunger turns to apathy and the person mentally wastes away. Celibacy always did leave a great deal to be desired!

Eileen Caddy:

> Stop sitting there with your hands folded looking on, doing
> nothing; Get into action and live this full and glorious life.
> Now. You have to do it.

If all you do is get up, go to work, come home and go to bed, then you develop a habit which, unless periodically changed, can turn into boredom. No matter how comfortable this pattern or routine starts to be, if it's not changed it will not satisfy. You need variety because if you get bored, you will tend to bore for Britain as well.

WARNING!

**As with all character traits, you have to strike
a balance between activity and rest. If you try
to juggle too many balls in the air, some are
bound to fall.**

THE BIG BOTTOM LINE

There are three types of people: those who make things happen, those who watch things happen and those who say 'What's happened?'

Guardian Angel 8:
DISCIPLINE

Lao Tse
(*The Character of Tao*):

> He who conquers others is strong; he who conquers himself is mighty.

Does it sometimes seem that mysterious forces are at work? Forces that delight in wreaking havoc with any efforts you make to take charge of your bad habits? Just when you resolve to balance your budget, that little black dress goes on sale. Just when you go on a diet, that mouthwatering Pizza pleads with you from the TV: 'Come hither and get a load of this, baby'. Of course, it is talking directly to your hips.

That little black dress goes on sale.

Call me old-fashioned, but I believe that much of the unhappiness and personal distress in the world is a result of failure to control tempers, appetites, passions and impulses. 'Oh, if only I had stopped myself' is the all too familiar refrain.

I find it gob smackingly hard to believe that people who are teaching self-esteem these days fail to link it with Discipline. Maybe it's because the word 'Discipline' smacks of Dickensian austerity and doesn't fit in with the feely, touchy world of psycho-speak.

In a valiant attempt to wash our self-esteem problems away in a warm bath of psycho-babble bubbles, modern therapists say we shouldn't criticise our undisciplined ways and resulting behaviour, that would be judgmental.

So what are they doing, encouraging us to endorse it? Giving us yet more excuses?

For anybody who doesn't think that discipline is vital to their character base, ponder this. How can you possibly start to build self-esteem if you don't have some mastery over yourself? Without discipline, how can you ever hope to build that bridge between you and your goals, between low and high self-esteem, life and living?

How Discipline Sets You Free

On the surface, it seems that discipline and freedom are opposites. You may think that discipline limits your options, forcing you to do things you never enjoy, whilst freedom implies a lack of boundaries and restrictions, enabling you to keep your options open.

Let's just say you go to the gym three times a week. In the past you probably thought that discipline was alien to your temperament, but, excuse me if I'm not mistaken, by going to the gym you are doing something that requires willpower and commitment. Thunderbolt city! It's your **Discipline** to exercise three times a week that is giving you freedom. Freedom from health problems, freedom to indulge in a little more food without whopping on some serious tonnage, freedom to feel energised so you can go on and do more, freedom to have a better life. It is Discipline that is actually setting you free and literally saving your life.

Julie Andrews:

> Some people regard discipline as a chore.
> For me, it is a kind of order that sets me free to fly.

The whole question of self-esteem lies at the heart of successful daily behaviour. If you want to be free of worry, guilt, jealousy and self-doubt, then you need self-discipline. Discipline affects your performance in every area of life. The woman with self-discipline can end pain as easily as she can create pleasure. Any self-discipline starts the process towards improved self-esteem.

Some Freedom Strategies

♥ **Avoid obvious sources of temptation.** Women who go window-shopping often end up buying more than the window. If eating at Burger King tempts you to forget your diet, then eat at home or go to a salad bar instead.

❤ **Place yourself in an environment in which desirable behaviour is likely to occur.** It may be difficult to force yourself to study, so how about rewarding yourself for time spent at the library?

❤ **Make unwanted behaviour impossible.** Tear up your credit cards so that you can't spend, and leave that cheesecake in the supermarket. You can't eat cake or even inhale it, if it's not sitting in the fridge at home trying to seduce you.

❤ **Exclude problem behaviour gradually from your environment.** For example, stop smoking first in the office, then while driving, then at home, etc.

Avoid obvious sources of temptation.

❤ **Engage in behaviours that are incompatible with bad habits.** Such as drinking a glass of water and a fattening milk-shake simultaneously. Grasping something firmly (ask his permission first) is a useful response to nail-biting.

❤ **Approach targets gradually through a series of painless steps.** Increase studying by five minutes a day. Putting out a ciggy that's only half-smoked.

❤ **Use Granny's method of no veggies, no dessert.** Carry out the grotty routine stuff before the favoured stuff. For example, don't watch TV unless you have studied first. Don't go out for dinner until you've been to the gym.

❤ **Make positive associations with your new behaviour.** See a healthy heart and an energised you every time you exercise or eat something that is good for you.

❤ **Create rewarding imagery for desired behaviour.** When you have achieved a goal, fantasise about all your friends patting you on the back or, better still, Kevin Costner patting you on the front.

Use Granny's method of no veggies, no dessert.

WARNING!

As with all things, exercise some common sense when it come to self-discipline. Don't confuse self-discipline with self-deprivation. Total abstinence and puritanical behaviour towards things like food, sex and shopping is not discipline, it's blatant S&M. The S&M control freak is the kind of girl that orders a McLettuce burger (and holds the bread); she's probably bulimic and endures having tubes put up her bum twice weekly for a good spring clean, while simultaneously living on a diet of mineral water (not fizzy because that can give you cellulite, darling).

Obsession with discipline is an addiction, *not* a healthy character trait.

Keep Practising the Healthy Habits

It takes discipline to form habits. Anyone can form new healthy habits in their life in order to feel better. We achieve our self-esteem in the same way that we learn to play the piano, solve maths problems or play tennis well, **THROUGH PRACTICE.**

Practice is the medicine so many people find hard to swallow. If it were easy, there would be no such thing as the multi-zillion pound diet industry which is specifically designed to make your wallet lighter and your bank balance slimmer! Of course, we can always enlist an army of trainers, therapists, support groups, step programmes, and other strategies, but in the end, it's practice that brings self-control.

The key to forming a habit is in the level of emotion at the beginning. The emotions need to be high so that you have the motivation to start a process and follow it through. You know, the kind of time after you get to bed at 5am having smoked 10 packets of cigarettes and drunk five bottles of Chateauneuf Du Plonka. You wake up, open your mouth and out fly a couple of parrots! You feel so goddamn lousy that you determine to give up the fags, right now! You never want to smell, let alone smoke, another one! That's the time to give up, but it takes discipline not to smoke that evening when you're back in the bar. Take heart, giving up becomes easier with practice.

Every new discipline affects all others. You become inspired to accept the next and the next. You've got to keep setting new disciplines for yourself if you want to build your self-esteem and, ultimately, have a happy life.

Keep reminding yourself, 'What do I want to look back on?' You may be able to postpone discipline in your life, but in the end you can't avoid it. Sooner or later, if you want to get anywhere or do anything to any extent, you have to practice self-discipline.

You get to bed at 5am having smoked 10 packets of cigarettes and drunk five bottles of Chateauneuf Du Plonka.

THE BIG BOTTOM LINE

You must have discipline; it is the bunch of keys that unlock all doors of awareness, goals, plans, joy, accomplishment and high self-worth. Without it, you will never unlock your potential. The pain of discipline is so much better than the pain of regret.

Guardian Angel 9:
HUMOUR

Colette

> Total absence of humour
> renders life impossible.

Being able to laugh at yourself is a security mechanism that allows you to defend yourself against the Assassins who attack your sanity. A sense of humour acts as a gaoler, able to set free your emotionally whacked out mind. If you are ever in a position where you think you are going to be robbed of your self-worth, apprehend, disarm and arrest the offending Assassin with some rapturous laughter. . .

IMMEDIATELY!

Humour, to me, has been a life-saving gift. As a base character trait, Humour is crucial to your happiness and long-term self-esteem. People don't laugh because their life is easy, but because they are givers and survivors. You have to increase your capacity for laughter, despair is too easy an option. The late comedienne **Marti Caine**, who died of cancer, used laughter to combat pain and occasionally terror. She said:

Despair is an easy option.

> So many people in show business, come from a deprived background; you've got to laugh otherwise you go mad. Adversity either breeds comedy or bitterness.

When she was diagnosed in 1989 as having malignant lymphoma, she was told that her life expectancy was 18 months, but she survived until 1995. She fought death with tenacious mirth. She joked about her illness and never evoked pity. 'The more you laugh the smaller it gets', she quipped on stage, 'if you don't mind me saying so, sir'.

By allowing yourself to see your own monstrous absurdities in a humourous light, you can actually stop yourself from going completely potty. Humour enables you to turn a negative situation into a different, more positive context altogether. It's a sort of confessional that heals, pardons and diminishes the negative thoughts.

On the whole women laugh more than men, mainly because we are better communicators; bigger talkers (no surprises there). But still none of us laugh as much as we should, which is a shame, because it has more health benefits than just about any other human behaviour. It's fun, it has no side-effects (except happiness) and it doesn't cost a penny. Time to take laughter a whole lot more seriously!

Why You Just Have to Laugh

Gail Parent:

> She knew what all smart women knew:
> laughter made you live better and longer.

If you can see the funny side of life then you have discovered one of the best prescriptions for longevity. Dr William Fry of the Stanford School of Medicine has studied the physical benefits of laughter and discovered that 100 laughs are equivalent to about ten minutes of jogging (without the sore boobs and stretch marks!). This is because regular laughter boosts the functioning of the body's most important systems, cardio-vascular, respiratory, hormonal, muscular, immune and central nervous system. Now who among us can't handle that for a bit of exercise?

Laughter also releases the body's natural painkillers, endorphins, a fact dramatically demonstrated by American journalist Norman Cousins who suffered from a painful spinal condition. He was desperately unhappy about his prognosis and transferred himself from his dreary hospital bed to a hotel. There he deliberately tried to cheer himself up by watching some of his favourite comedy films and reading books of humour by some of his favourite comedy writers.

Not only did he feel happier in his hotel room, but he also produced scientific evidence to his doctors that his laughter had a useful and practical effect on his physical condition. Cousins found that five minutes of laughter gave him two hours of pain relief by reducing the inflammations in his body. To all intents and purposes, he had laughed himself better.

Doctors are now convinced that laughter really *is* the best medicine and to put this concept to the test, a Humour Centre was recently set up in America to treat people who are at a high risk of developing cancer. Their theory is that the

Laugh yourself better.

body changes when you laugh and the disease-fighting white blood cells become more active. The actual 'ha ha ha' action of laughter forces carbon dioxide out of the lungs and draws in more oxygen, improving air quality in our body and making it less prone to disease. Hearty laughter also exercises and relaxes muscles in the face, shoulders, abdomen and diaphragm.

Marcelle D'Argy Smith (Columnist, former editor of *Cosmopolitan, You Magazine* 5 July 1996):

> I never felt stressed, yet at one time I got so phobic that I couldn't cross over Regent Street. My remedy is always to make someone else laugh. There's a funny side to everything: divorce, disaster, disease, despair, you just have to look for it. Laughter is a great healer.

Humour helps divert attention from your problems. Laughter isn't only a pleasant experience, it's also a positive, natural phenomenon which helps ensure that the body benefits fully.

How We Lose Our Sense of Humour

The worst thing about a failing sense of humour is that we grow up, live and work but we stop playing. The progress of laughter through our lives follows a similar pattern for everyone. A baby first chuckles at the age of three months and from then onwards the rate of laughter increases until the age of six years, by which time the average child chortles 300 times a day.

As we get older, we are taught not to lose control and many people are scared to laugh because of this fact. 'Don't giggle in class'; 'No laughing at the dinner table'. As a result we become progressively more sombre until we reach adulthood, when the young at heart may still manage to force out about 100 spurious laughs a day, while the Moaning Minnies of this world grumble by on a mere six or so. Pathetic really!

Are you referring to flatulence?

When probed as to the last time they let rip, most people will merely look baffled and assume you are referring to flatulence. That's because most of us girls are not even aware when we laugh, we laugh as a reflex, when we're nervous or short of anything to say and often at things that aren't even funny.

We can of course smile on demand, as many a stiff upper-lipped family portrait can testify, but as for laughing on demand, well that would be a bit like faking an orgasm! You can induce many things, but it's hard with laughter, because real laughter is something that you burst into with complete spontaneity. False laughter just isn't convincing at all.

Humour is a Choice

If we want to start to get that *joie de vivre* back into our lives, we must choose to have it. We have to start to see our disasters as harmless, engaging and rather amusing little numbers, otherwise we can fall apart. Let's assume that you have pranged your boss's new car; the waiter's just dropped avocado prawn cocktail down your new silk dress and your best friend isn't speaking to you because you suggested she gets a nose job.

Now, under the circumstances, you have a choice of reaction:

1 Laugh like a drain.

2 Blub for two weeks.

3 Throw yourself under a train.

You might well feel on the verge of (3), particularly if the Character Assassins have been tampering with your humour mechanism and have caused it to fail. However from personal experience I can tell you that (1) is by far the healthiest option.

WARNING!

Before I learned to laugh I frowned a lot and my eyebrows used to knit together on a regular basis. My forehead now resembles corrugated cardboard. Suggestion: If you don't want to look like a bulldog by the time you are 30. . . start laughing now.

Ways to Put More Laughter Back into Your Life

First, try to spend as much time as possible with cheerful, happy people. If you spend your time with people who have long faces, eventually you'll acquire their black views on life. Depression is contagious. Such people blunt the happiness of their families and they cast an emotional cloud over what should be a happy time. Avoid them at all costs and spend as much time as possible with people who laugh and enjoy life to the full. It's a much better pill to swallow than Prozac.

Secondly, don't take yourself too seriously. Many people with responsible jobs feel that they have to maintain a serious demeanour at all times. Wrong! You will lose nothing by allowing yourself to laugh occasionally. I love that line of Melanie Griffiths in *Working Girl* when asked what she's going to do with her life after she gets fired from her job: *'I'm gonna wise up and not take the whole thing so seriously'.*

So many of us take our jobs too seriously. If you let yourself have a bit of fun, then you will stop stressing yourself out; people will still respect you and, heavens above, they may even like you better.

Thirdly, make a list of favourite funny films and books. Make up your own video library for hours of genuine relaxation. Keep on hand for a bad day the books that really amuse you. The strange thing is that when you've got something you can rely on to cheer you up, then you hardly ever need to rely on it.

Agnes Repplier:

> Humour brings insight and tolerance.

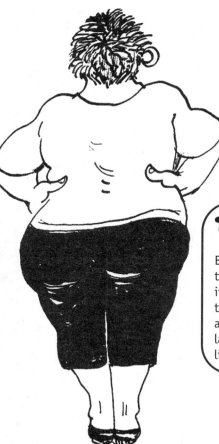

THE BIG BOTTOM LINE

Being happy is a decision that you have to take, your sanity and health depend on it. I'm not saying that we should spend the rest of our lives rolling around in the aisles and splitting our corsets with laughter at the first signs of disaster, just lighten up a little.

Guardian Angel 10:
FRIENDSHIP

The quality of your life is very much dependent upon your ability to form deep and long-term relationships, with yourself and with others. The Principle that allows you to form these relationships is Friendship. Friendship is the outer display of the inner values of integrity, loyalty, honesty, compassion, sincerity and trust.

Practically every aspect of your life involves you relating to other people. When people are on their deathbeds surrounded by their loved ones they say things like, 'Take good care of your brother, look after your father'. Nobody regrets that they didn't spend more time at the office, or the Harrods sale: all they talk about is the quality of their relationships.

Friendships are inextricably linked to self-esteem and happiness because many of us judge ourselves as a direct result of how we get on with other people. When things are going well, you tend to feel good and your self-esteem is high. But, oh dear, when you're having problems. . . time to eat a box of Kleenex!

> *Friendship, like home, is where we go when nobody else will have us*

What Attacks Friendships?

You guessed it.. . . Character Assassins! They use every tool in their arsenal of weaponry to scupper all your attempts at cementing close relationships.

Wild Expectations: 'If you loved me you'd buy me two dozen roses every week.'

Limiting Self-Belief: 'I'm so worthless, that there's no way you could ever love me.' You know the score. All of these insecurities attack the heart of friendships, creating an environment of mistrust, disloyalty, jealously, dishonesty and a lack of integrity. Life gets pretty lonely once this happens.

It takes more than a healthy sense of self-esteem and successful potty training to earn the friendship of others. In order to have a friend you must first be a friend. You need to focus on what really matters, the person you are. You will never, ever be able to win friends and influence them until you first display the same traits that you would want them to display.

How Do I Become a Friend?

Maybe you already know the answer to this question. But in case you don't I'll tell you anyway. The two absolutely foot stomping, table banging, 'must' ingredients, if any of your friendships are going to stand a chance of surviving, are:

1: Trust

2: Compassion

Note: **If you have to choose between a good reputation and great wealth, choose the former.**

Trust

Erma J Fisk:

We all live on bases of shifting sands, (and) need trust.

Whom do we trust in life? People who are trustworthy! Every social activity, every human enterprise requiring people to interact together is impeded when people don't trust each other. When we are perceived to be trustworthy, others are likely to be more honest and open with us. This, of course, works both ways.

> *Be true to your word, your work and your friend*

A trustworthy person has self-respect as well as the respect of others. How is trust cultivated? Like most principles it is best developed and exercised in harmony with others.

Suggestion: Keep secrets.

Compassion

Sharon Stone: *Hello Magazine* September 96

> There's only one way to live. If you are not living as a loving individual, you're not living the truth.

George Eliot once asked, 'What do we live for if it is not to make life less difficult for each other?' Given the importance of compassion in building friendships, promoting happiness, and making the world go round it's surprising that so few of us practice it. Maybe this is because in a new era of psychoanalysis we have spawned the **me, I, myself** generation which has very little room for compassion. 'Look after Number One' is a very popularist attitude and 'everybody else will be all right'. But they are not all right, are they? We live in a traumatic world of war, starvation, failing education standards and homeless people, not to mention a proliferation of the decisive -*ism's:* racism, sexism, chauvinism and the rest.

Being compassionate is **not about self-sacrifice or taking responsibility for everyone.** Compassion is simply a virtue that considers the lives, emotions and circumstances of other people. It is an active orientation towards fellowship and sharing, towards companionship in distress or hardship. It means being able to say to someone 'What are you going through?'

> *The love in your heart wasn't put there to stay.*
> *Love isn't love till you give it away*

You're probably thinking, how the hell can I brim over with benevolence when I feel so depleted myself? Surprisingly, giving without expecting any kind of return in your life can make you feel fantastic. The more you give the better you will feel and the more abundance keeps popping back into your life. In fact, very soon giving and receiving become the exact same thing. It is through your involvement with the

How the hell can i brim over with benevolence when i feel so depleted myself?

world that makes you truly belong.

Eileen Caddy:

> You find true joy and happiness in life when you give and give and go on giving and never count the cost.

Modern day therapy is crazy, emphasising the inner soul and ignoring the outer soul, because this supports the decline of the world. As Sendivogius, an alchemist said, *'The greater part of the soul lies on the outside of the body'.* Being compassionate can have a ripple effect and spread to your entire community. Every healthy friendship you nurture moves you further away from unhealthy patterns. No matter whom this relationship is with, your further relationships will be better for it . . . and so will you.

No matter whom this relationship is with.

Suggestion: Practice kindness. If you're queuing to pay to get out of the car park, pay for the person behind you as well. Or if you're in a café, buy coffee anonymously for the woman who has just struggled in with a screaming toddler and a parking ticket. Imagine the knock-on effect this would have. You can't commit a random act of kindness without feeling as if your own troubles have been lightened or that the world has become a better place.

> *Perfect kindness acts without thinking of kindness*

Friendship Accelerators

1. Forgiveness

Hannah Arendt:

Forgiveness is the key to action and freedom.

An important part of friendship is forgiveness. There isn't one single person living who hasn't been hurt by the mistakes of key people in their lives, and we have all hurt others in the past. Keeping a score of these incidents just sets us up for bucket-loads of blame and resentment, trapping you in the past and victimising you in the present. Forgiveness, on the other hand, sets you free.

However, forgiveness does not excuse bad behaviour. For example, like the time you played the Angel Gabriel

Forgiveness does not excuse bad behaviour.

in the school nativity play and little Johnny Smith put a whoopee cushion on your seat, the full impact of which was heard when you sat down after your rendering of *Wind Beneath My Wings*. Nor does it mean thumbs up approval: 'what a gas, must remember that one for his wedding'. Rather, it involves a willingness to understand with compassion.

All forgiveness means is that you have decided to deal with your negative feelings, put them behind you and moved on. The person who hurt you probably did so because of his own shortcomings and you did not deserve it. Only you can make the decision to let go of the chains that bind you and put them to rest forever. Forgiveness is an act, not a process, you don't have to make a meal of it. You just want to lighten the load.

2. Sensitivity

Erma Bombeck:

A friend doesn't go on a diet because you are fat. A friend never defends a husband who gets his wife an electric skillet for her birthday. A friend will tell you she saw your old boyfriend, and he's a priest.

Being sensitive and considerate towards others will take you further in life than any college or professional degree. Failing to register another's feelings is a major deficit in your character as well as a tragic failing in what it means to be human. At the root of all human relationships is emotional atonement and the capacity for empathy. The best way to build rapport is to treat everyone you meet as you would like to be treated.

Cynthia Heimel:

> Those of us who have the situation in Lebanon in perspective and know exactly how to plot a Gay Rights campaign are usually morons. We bark at our kids when they have innocent homework questions. We don't notice when our lover has deadlines. We forget to call our best friend back when she's had root canal.

'Homework deadlines' and 'root canal' are the important things in life, and only when we have these small issues and dramas taken care of, do we have time to look at the larger questions.

Suggestion: Remember birthdays, anniversaries, job interviews, driving tests, exams, ringing your friend to wish her luck with her new date.

3. Compliments

Oscar Wilde:

> Ah, now-a-days we are all of us so hard up, that the only pleasant things to pay are compliments. They're the only things that we can pay.

Don't you just love it when somebody says to you, totally unprompted, 'wow, you look gorgeous' or 'I can't believe you did that, it's amazing'. It gives you an enormous surge of pleasure, that bottom-tingly feeling. I ask you, who the hell doesn't want to feel important?

Everybody likes to be told they are doing well, that they are beautiful, clever, amazing. But do we get told enough? Of course not. None of us ever gets enough compliments.

So, if you want to build a few bridges and influence people, compliment your friends. You don't have to be a crawler or heap on insincere sentiment.

Just recognise their good points and let them know. Not only do they feel good but so do you. Express, don't impress. Express builds a bridge, impress builds a gulf.

WARNING!

DON'T MAJOR IN MINORS

Being a good friend is the number one criteria for friendship. However, your choice of friends is absolutely crucial to your happiness. Good friends bring you up and bad friends pull you down.

It's a simple fact that you become like the people you associate with. This is because subconsciously you are influenced by the attitudes and actions of those you spend time with. If you are around people who are negative or depressed the chances are that you become negative and depressed. If you hang out with dorks, you become a dork, and so on.

You become a dork.

Evaluate everybody who resides within your circle of influence and ask, what are they doing to me? What have they got me saying, doing, listening to, talking about? How is this affecting my self-esteem?

If you really want high self-esteem you've got to surround yourself with the right people. Those who always seem positive, and who have a good sense of humour, as opposed to drama queens who wallow in negativity?

Intimate Friendships

You need to build friendships before you build intimate relationships. Every boyfriend, partner or spouse you have will affect you and influence you. Make sure that you want their type of influence.

There is absolutely no doubt that the quality of your personal long-term relationships depends on compassionate love as opposed to romantic love, otherwise it cannot be sustained in a healthy fashion. Ask yourself 'do I have genuine concern for the issues that cause the other person concern?' Relationships are not just about serial snogging sessions and ripping his underpants off with your teeth every two minutes.

> *Love is not measured by how many times we touch each other, but by how many times we reach each other*

However, romantic love does happen (apparently), and in a flash we can become totally vulnerable and infantile over somebody that we are in love with. The metaphorical romantic gesture, the dropped handkerchief, the declaration of passionate desire. **But** the triumphant twang of a bed spring is <u>not enough</u> to sustain a relationship and many people fall romantically in love with a deliberately constructed persona. No friendship built on such a sad foundation can last much more than a fortnight.

Margate Anderson:

In real love you want the other person's good. In romantic love you want the other person.

Soon, initial idealised passions will give way to objective recognition of differences in attitudes and interests. Things you didn't guess were inside either of you will come out, including the fact that he talks with his mouth full and his feet smell like Stilton cheese. Meanwhile you go in for the emotional kill: 'If you really loved me you'd never see your mother again, score me some drugs, repaint the house', you name it.

Berscheid and Walster (1978) suggest that people are much more likely to maintain a relationship once romance begins to fade if they have developed compassionate love. Compassionate love requires trust, loyalty, sharing of feelings, mutual respect, a lack of being hypercritical and a willingness to sacrifice. Compassionate love is based on genuine knowledge of the other person, not idealisation.

If compassionate love blooms then a relationship can survive the fading extremes of romance. At this point a couple can work together to meet each other's sexual as well as compassionate needs. Skills can substitute for the excitement of novelty.

Sounds suspiciously like friendship to me.

THE BIG BOTTOM LINE

All relationships, whether with yourself, personal, social or business, are based on the same two global criteria, **TRUST** and **COMPASSION.** This signifies true friendship and there are absolutely no other substitutes for these two traits if any type of long-term relationship is to succeed.

Now you have met the Angels, the true Guardians of your Character, you probably realise that there is nothing you need that you don't already have, in order to be happy.

From now on you need to live each day as if you would climb a mountain. An occasional glance toward the summit will keep your goal in mind. There will be shadows, but this will be balanced by many beautiful scenes bathed in light.

Do yourself a favour as you walk up this mountain called life. Climb slowly and steadily enjoying each passing moment and take some time to really see. Take a moment to look at what is going on around you, right where you are. Awareness of your pattern is all you need to sustain you along the way.

To get a clear view of how your progress might fare as you move toward your final destination I am now going to take you to the **Mountain of Clarity**. A fitting climax for the end of this journey.

THE MOUNTAIN OF
CLARiTY

Welcome to the Mountain of Clarity.

Part 5:
The Mountain of Clarity

Welcome home!

You have finally made it, **Back on Top**. It probably seems a long time since you started on your journey, but think how much you have achieved and what you have passed along the way. By dealing with each new challenge, overcoming it, you unleash within yourself a new kind of freedom and power and a capacity to soar heights previously undreamed of. There were probably times when you felt sure you would not be able to vanquish the Assassins, they may have seemed just too strong. But then you did and you found yourself at the Gate. By throwing back the bolts and entering the City of Happiness you have made yourself so much stronger and more able to deal with life's little 'jokes'. Pilgrim's progress indeed! It is often the vision of a distant destination that keeps us motivated, but it is the journey itself that matters in the end.

By reading this book you have responded to the challenge to develop your character and moved up to a better place with a better vantage point from which to survey your life. From here the limits of your own field of vision are wider. Let these be your limits for the world.

A journey from Doom City to Happiness is more than a journey of discovery, it is the understanding of certain principles and the *progressive* development of your character. It is going to take some time for you to exercise and develop the strengths your Guardian Angels have bestowed on you, these principles need regularly dusting down and taking off the shelf to make them work properly. And the greatest thing of all is that the quality of your life is completely within your hands.

The View from the Top

Everybody who has made it to the top of the Mountain should be happy with themselves. Strengthened with resolve and brimming with self-esteem. Congratulations, *you* are one of that happy gang!

Now you're up there, keep focusing clearly on what really matters: the kind of person *you are*. Building self-esteem and becoming happy is all about being proactive, a word which means, literally, *for* activity, rather than against it. You've got to get out there and kick the proverbial backside of life in order to keep the 10 Guardian Angels at the centre of your life.

Keep Watching Out for those Assassins!

Don't underestimate the power of the Assassins. They will never miss an opportunity to home in on your more vulnerable moments. But they will find it harder and harder to get to you as the defensive mechanisms of the Angels become firmly embedded as part of your psyche.

Break away from the negative pull of the Character Assassins NOW!

Nothing sinks people faster than negative beliefs and behaviour.

Watch out for:

♥ **Negative Self-Beliefs:** They assassinate your character. Choose only those beliefs that support you, which give you hope, confidence and energy.

♥ **Negative Self-Talk**
Don't say anything to yourself that you wouldn't say to a cherished friend.

♥ **Foolish Expectations:** They will kidnap you from the real world and hold you prisoner in a city of illusion and disappointment. Take steps to adjust them so that they help you become happy.

♥ **Poisonous Patterns:** Poisonous patterns of behaviour keep you locked into low self-esteem and unhappiness. Progress has no greater enemy, so find them and break them!

Turn away from the Assassins in order to move towards the principles (the Angels) that strengthen your character. What have you got to lose but the shackles of the despair, unhappiness, dissatisfaction and low self-esteem of your past?

Your life is worth more than mere fodder for the Character Assassins to devour and regurgitate.

Open the 'Gate' - Unleash Your Power!

This book is the sword which can cut you free of the bonds our Assassins have bound us in. Unlock those unique human skills which will help you to distinguish between reality and illusion, to transform your life and release you into the city of Angels and Happiness.

Throw back those Bolts and Unlock the Gate!

💙 **Self-Awareness:** so that you can get some kind of perspective on your life. Be aware of the social and psychic cycles within you.

💙 **Choice:** so that in the future you can take actions which are based on empowering principles rather than on negative thoughts, moods and circumstances. You are not a victim. You are not the product of your past. You are the product of your choices today.

💙 **Reason:** Get rid of numbing complacency. Don't wait for a crisis to stir you into action. Be proactive.

It's a great feeling when you have obtained total mastery of these three Bolts. But don't try to jump the gun. You cannot get to the Angels before you have created a new way of thinking about old problems. Nor can you vanquish the Assassins immediately after passing through the Gate. Do everything in the correct order *and you cannot fail.*

Summon the Angels

Like a novelty codpiece, you can't keep a good character down. Once you're on the up, there is only one way to continue, *up, up, up!*

We already have the principles of happy living embedded deep within us. To achieve the highest level of life fulfilment, learn to select, understand and condition the messages of the Angels into character traits that build self-esteem and then commit to live by them every single day. Let's look at the principles, our Guardian Angels, once again.

❤ **Responsibility:** Take charge of yourself right now. The only person with primary responsibility for your future is you.

❤ **Courage:** Don't wait until you can be a big heroine in some dire crisis. Small, daily events also require courage. Start *now.*

❤ **Health:** Breathe properly, eat the right foods, get sufficient rest and exercise regularly. Without energy and vitality, you can't do a thing.

❤ **Competence:** Competence builds self-esteem. Develop it for yourself, no one else.

❤ **Purpose:** Purpose fills you with a deep certainty, energy, vision, and strength. If you don't have purpose in place then all your actions will be meaningless.

❤ **Identity:** Know who you are and be what you are, because this is the real key to becoming better than you are.

❤ **Activity:** Become a 'doer' and make things happen. Examine not what you do for a living, but what you do *with* your living.

❤ **Discipline:** Without discipline, you will never unlock and discover your potential. Discipline helps to build that bridge between you and your goals, between low and high self-esteem and life and living.

❤ **Humour:** Be able to laugh at yourself, it's the strongest defence you have against the Assassins.

❤ **Friendship:** True friendship is the outer display of the inner values of integrity, loyalty, honesty, compassion, sincerity and trust. The quality of your life is dependent upon these values.

Keep the Balance of Focus

> *All principles are like bonfires.*
> *They fizzle out when unattended*

You must work on developing all 10 principles of self-esteem regularly in wise and balanced ways through practising them every day. They are all as important as each other. If any of these principles remain undeveloped, you may be creating a black hole that devours your energy and attention. If you think of your self-esteem as the spider in the centre of its web, if a hole suddenly developed not only would the spider not catch any flies, he would probably fall through the hole to his doom. It's the same with principles. Work on repairing any gaps in your confidence, spin away and you will soon have once again a strong and defensive web of self-esteem.

WARNING!

You might well be tempted to think that success in developing one principle into a character trait could compensate for failure in developing others. Go to the back of the class! Think about it, can a stronger personal identity compensate for the fact there is no purpose in your life? No way.

High self-esteem on a consistent and sustained basis requires balance. Work on developing each principle into a conditioned character trait, through weekly goals. Always monitor and reward your progress.

Action

The best time to take action is when the desire is hot and the emotion is strong. If you're feeling strong and motivated then **GO FOR iT.**

Action pronto!

Faye Dunaway: *Sunday Times* 1st September 96

> As an actress it's fascinating to find out what makes you
> tick and why, but it doesn't necessarily help. The only
> thing that will change you is <u>clarity</u> and some kind of
> <u>action</u>. I need to come up with any tricks I can, for
> instance to stop being late.

You Can Do It

Believe that you can do all this stuff. Why shouldn't you be the best you can be? Nobody else can do it after all. Who wants to be mediocre? That kind of person doesn't end up feeling great at the end of the day. Make a splash, not a ripple.

It Takes Time

> *Progress has little to do with speed,*
> *but much to do with direction*

It takes time to comprehend the principles of the Angels. You need to slow down to sense them and let them in. Just like a new friend, you need time to get to know each another.

And yes, there are times when you will get frustrated. There are no quick-fix methods for achieving character develop-ment. It would be totally irresponsible of me to suggest your transformation will be instantaneous. It won't be. But it will happen. You just need to build gradually and daily, just as you would if you were trying to get physically fit after years of idleness. Every day you need to gain perspective then make some decisions in the light of that perspective.

You'll probably find that the progress you experience comes in surges, followed by periods of consolidation. By taking small steps, one at a time, we will soon feel a sense of progress. And then guess what, **time flies.**

Good Luck . . .

Every great journey begins with the first step. When you finally get on your way you will find that your progress through the City of Happiness is like getting on to a bus that you can't get off. Once you're on it, you ride on and on. This momentum will help you make your life what you want it to be. If you do this, the success you achieve will lead to your dreams being realised. If you know you want it, *have* it.

GOOD LUCK, Fellow Pilgrim!

Oprah Winfrey

I'm finally ready to own my own power; to say, all right, this is who I am.

If you like it, you like it. And if you don't, you don't. So watch out, I'm gonna fly.